PRAY I
FA

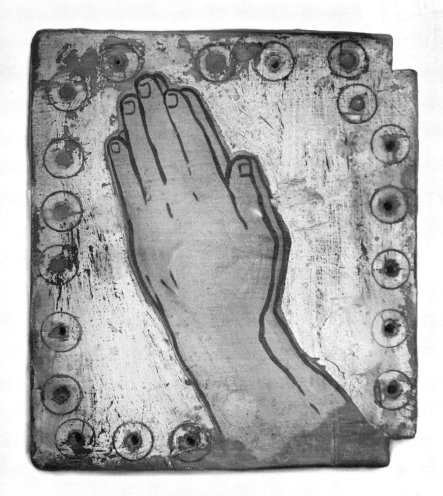

T.W. HUNT *and*
CLAUDE KING

LifeWay Press®
Nashville, Tennessee

ISBN 978-1-4158-5284-2
Item 005035525

Dewey decimal classification: 248.3
Subject heading: PRAYER

This book is a resource for course CG-1255 in the subject area
Prayer in the Christian Growth Study Plan.

Cover illustration: Mac Premo

To order additional copies of this resource, write to LifeWay Church Resources
Customer Service; One LifeWay Plaza; Nashville, TN 37234-0113; fax (615) 251-5933;
phone toll free (800) 458-2772; order online at *www.lifeway.com;*
e-mail *orderentry@lifeway.com;* or visit the LifeWay Christian Store serving you.

Printed in the United States of America

Leadership and Adult Publishing
LifeWay Church Resources
One LifeWay Plaza
Nashville, TN 37234-0175

Contents

Introducing T. W. Hunt and Claude King 4
Let's Learn to Pray Together 5

Week 1: Six Kinds of Prayer 8
Day 1: Prayer Is a Relationship 10
Day 2: Responding and Asking Prayers 12
Day 3: Four Kinds of Responding Prayers 14
Day 4: Two Kinds of Asking Prayers 16
Day 5: Praying with Others 18

Week 2: Developing Your Prayer Life 20
Day 1: Reasons to Pray 22
Day 2: Daily Prayer 24
Day 3: Tools to Help You Pray 26
Day 4: The Bible and Prayer 28
Day 5: Being a House of Prayer 30

Week 3: Responding Prayers 32
Day 1: Confession 34
Day 2: Praise 36
Day 3: Worship 38
Day 4: Thanksgiving 40
Day 5: Responding Together 42

Week 4: Asking Prayers 44
Day 1: Praying for Yourself and Others 46
Day 2: Reasons God Answers Prayer 48
Day 3: Reasons God Doesn't Answer Prayer 50
Day 4: Principles for Asking 52
Day 5: Agreeing Together 54

Week 5: Petition 58
Day 1: Asking for Yourself 60
Day 2: A Model for Petition 62

Day 3: Following Your Father's Leading 64
Day 4: Praying for Yourself 66
Day 5: Asking Others to Pray for You 68

Week 6: Intercession 70
Day 1: Asking for Others 72
Day 2: Examples of Intercession 74
Day 3: Following Your Master's Leading 76
Day 4: Praying for Others 78
Day 5: Praying Together in God's Work 80

Leader Guide 82
Session 1: Six Kinds of Prayer 85
Session 2: Developing Your Prayer Life 86
Session 3: Responding Prayers 87
Session 4: Asking Prayers 88
Session 5: Petition 89
Session 6: Intercession 90

Discipleship Helps
Six Kinds of Prayer 91
Prayers of Confession 92
Prayers of Praise 94
Prayers of Worship 96
Prayers of Thanksgiving 98
Prayers of Petition 100
Prayers of Intercession 102
Daily Requests 104
Weekly Requests 105
Monthly Requests 108
Suggestions for Praying Together 110

Christian Growth Study Plan 111
The Growing Disciples Series 112
Scripture-Memory Cards 113

Introducing
T. W. Hunt and Claude King

T. W. Hunt has given much of his life to teaching others the ways of the Lord. For 24 years he taught music and missions at Southwestern Baptist Theological Seminary in Fort Worth, Texas. For seven years prior to his retirement, T. W. served as a prayer consultant for the Sunday School Board of the Southern Baptist Convention (now LifeWay Christian Resources). He was a member of the Bold Mission Prayer Thrust Team that issued a call to prayer and solemn assembly on September 17, 1989. He is a graduate of Ouachita Baptist College and holds master of music and doctor of philosophy degrees from North Texas State University. He is married to his childhood sweetheart, Laverne. They have one daughter, Melana; six grandchildren; and two great-grandchildren. T. W. and Laverne make their home in Spring, Texas. In addition to numerous articles, T. W. has written several books, including *Music in Missions: Discipling Through Music, The Life-Changing Power of Prayer, Disciple's Prayer Life: Walking in Fellowship with God* (with Catherine Walker), *The Mind of Christ* (with Claude King), and *From Heaven's View* (with daughter Melana).

Claude King is an editor in chief for leadership and adult undated resources at LifeWay Christian Resources. In 1990 he coauthored *Experiencing God: Knowing and Doing the Will of God* with Henry Blackaby, which has sold more than six million copies and has been translated into more than 60 languages. Prior to returning to LifeWay in 2005, he served as a prayer strategy coordinator for New Hope New York in New York City. Claude serves on the board of directors for Final Command Ministries. A graduate of Belmont College and New Orleans Baptist Theological Seminary, he is married to Reta and has two daughters and one grandson. Some of the other LifeWay courses he has written or coauthored include: *Come to the Lord's Table, The Call to Follow Christ, Fresh Encounter: Seeking God Together for Revival in the Land, The Mind of Christ,* and *Made to Count Life Planner.*

Let's Learn to Pray Together

Genuine prayer is not a religious ritual for Christians to practice a few times each day. Prayer is a relationship God has with His children in which we talk with our Heavenly Father. Prayer is a time for us to enter the presence of the Creator and Ruler of the universe to understand what is on His mind and heart. Prayer is a holy privilege made possible by the sacrifice of Jesus Christ on our behalf. We have prepared this course for two purposes:

1. To help you develop a meaningful, well-balanced, and daily prayer life. You will understand and use the following six kinds of prayer in your daily prayer life:

PRAYER	NATURE OF THE PRAYER	GOD
Confession	Responding to …	God's holiness
Praise	Responding to …	God's attributes
Worship	Responding to …	God's glory
Thanksgiving	Responding to …	God's riches
Petition	Asking that is led by …	Your Heavenly Father
Intercession	Asking that is led by …	Your Master

2. To help you pray effectively with other believers. God has made a special promise about praying together: "If two of you on earth agree about any matter that you pray for, it will be done for you by My Father in heaven. For where two or three are gathered together in My name, I am there among them" (Matthew 18:19-20). Although this promise appears in the context of restoring a straying brother, it applies to any united prayer of Christians. God desires that His people reflect the unity that is part of His nature (see John 17:11). Therefore, God promises great authority to prayers of agreement among believers where that unity is fostered. God also promises a greater dimension of His presence when two or three meet to pray. We want you to experience the joy, power, and intimacy united prayer brings. Praying together, however, is not just adding together several individual prayers in sequence. Praying together effectively is a conversation among believers and God. Learning to pray together will be a most rewarding adventure in learning what God Himself is like.

STUDYING THIS COURSE

This six-week study consists of two important components:

1. Individual study. You will study individual lessons five days each week. Study only one lesson each day and use what you are learning in your daily prayer life. Each lesson should take from 10 to 15 minutes. You may choose, however, to spend more time in personal prayer. Do not omit the learning activities. They are designed to help you learn and apply what you study. They should help enrich your personal prayer experiences. Unless you have an introductory session, you should plan to study week 1 prior to your first group session.

2. Small-group prayer. You will join one or more other believers in a weekly prayer group. The time you spend together will not be a time just to talk about prayer. It primarily will be a prayer meeting in which you apply what you are learning by praying together. Your small group could consist of you and your spouse, family, friends, Christian business associates, fellow participants in a prayer ministry, class, or ongoing study group. By meeting with other believers for prayer, you will learn to pray more effectively. If you struggle with praying aloud, give this group experience a try anyway. By learning to pray in your personal study during the week, you will be better prepared to verbalize your prayers. Learning to pray along with others can be a deeply rewarding experience.

A Testimony of United Prayer

In 1744 pastors in Scotland began to promote unity in prayer for revival. They were led to this action because of the poor state of God's church and the immoral world around them. They sensed that God was leading them to call for united, extraordinary prayer for an outpouring of God's glory and a demonstration of His love and grace toward all people.

The original call to prayer invited persons to set aside time on Saturday evening and Sunday morning every week for prayer in private groups, public meetings, and individually. The proposal also invited persons to set aside the whole day or part of a day the first Tuesday of each quarter for solemn prayer. If urgent circumstances prevented a person's attendance, the individual was encouraged to devote the next available day to private prayer.

After two years the pastors agreed to continue and enlarge participation in these prayer unions. They sent a proposal to fellow ministers abroad. As a result, prayer concerts began to spread in Scotland, England, Wales, Ireland, and North America. Jonathan Edwards, a pastor in New England, was so moved by the appeal that he wrote a long letter challenging Christians everywhere to join in the prayer concerts.

In 1784 Edwards's letter had a profound influence on ministers in the Northampton Association in England. This association issued to its 20 churches the Call to Prayer of 1784. The call invited individuals and groups to join in concerted prayer on the first Monday of each month. The objective of the united prayer was to see an outpouring of the Holy Spirit on God's people and the spread of the gospel throughout the world. Following is the text of the call.

> The grand object in prayer is to be that the Holy Spirit may be poured down on our ministers and churches, that sinners may be converted, the saints edified, the interest of religion revived, and the name of God glorified. At the same time, remember, we trust you will not confine your requests to your own societies, or to your own immediate connection; let the whole interest of the Redeemer be affectionately remembered, and the spread of the Gospel to the most distant parts of the habitable globe be the object of your most fervent requests.[1]

The prayer concerts were so meaningful that the next year the association voted to continue the prayer concerts. Neighboring associations joined this movement, which began to spread across denominational lines. By 1792 the Second Great Awakening began to break out in England. Word of this revival spread across the Atlantic, and in 1794 Isaac Backus and other ministers in New England extended a similar call to prayer. By 1797 the revival fires began to break out in the United States.

One lasting benefit of the Call to Prayer of 1784 is the development of the modern missions movement. William Carey was saved and baptized just nine months before the call to prayer was issued and had begun to preach in the Northampton Association. After eight years of these prayer concerts for "the spread of the Gospel to the most distant parts of the habitable globe," Carey wrote his famous "Enquiry into the Obligations of Christians to Use Means for the Conversion of the Heathen." That year he helped organize the English Baptist Missionary Society. The next year he left for India as its first missionary. Throughout history every major missions movement has been preceded by a corresponding major prayer movement.

When God calls His people to return to Him and they respond in repentance and united prayer, God is able to bring the revival He desires of us. When God's people begin to pray for the Kingdom work of bringing the lost to Christ, God calls many as laborers in His harvest. Our nation and the world have reached a desperate point, and again we need to hear God's call to *explicit agreement* through *visible union* in *extraordinary prayer*. Let's learn to pray together and join God's work of transforming our nation and our world for His glory.

---

1. *Ter-Jubilee Celebrations* (London: Baptist Missionary Society, 1942–44), 21.

Week 1

Six Kinds of Prayer

"If you believe, you will receive
whatever you ask for in prayer."
Matthew 21:22

Six Kinds of Prayer

OVERVIEW OF WEEK 1
Day 1: Prayer Is a Relationship
Day 2: Responding and Asking Prayers
Day 3: Four Kinds of Responding Prayers
Day 4: Two Kinds of Asking Prayers
Day 5: Praying with Others

VERSE TO MEMORIZE
"If you believe, you will receive whatever you ask for in prayer" (Matthew 21:22).

DISCIPLESHIP HELPS FOR WEEK 1
"Six Kinds of Prayer" (p. 91)
"Prayers of Confession" (pp. 92–93)
"Suggestions for Praying Together" (p. 110)

PREVIEW OF WEEK 1
This week you will—
• overview this six-week study;
• understand that the nature of prayer is an intimate love relationship with God;
• understand that God wants you to identify with Him by becoming like Him and
  by participating with Him in His work;
• understand and begin using the following six kinds of prayer in your daily prayer life.
  —Confession: responding to God's holiness
  —Praise: responding to God's attributes
  —Worship: responding to God's glory
  —Thanksgiving: responding to God's riches
  —Petition: asking that is led by your Heavenly Father
  —Intercession: asking that is led by your Master

Day 1 • Prayer Is a Relationship

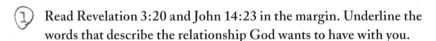

 As you begin each day's lesson, read the prayer promise in the left margin and begin your study with prayer. Today's prayer promise is also your Scripture-memory verse for this week. Ask the Lord to teach you how to pray with this kind of faith that secures His answer.

Scripture-Memory Verse
"If you believe, you will receive whatever you ask for in prayer" (Matthew 21:22).

Prayer is not one-sided communication with a distant God. Prayer is a conversation between you and God, a relationship between you and your Creator. God desires your fellowship. More than anything else, He wants you to love Him with all your being (see Deuteronomy 6:5 in the margin). He also wants you to know and experience His love and presence. God is seeking that kind of relationship with you!

Deuteronomy 6:5
"Love the LORD your God with all your heart, with all your soul, and with all your strength."

1) Read Revelation 3:20 and John 14:23 in the margin. Underline the words that describe the relationship God wants to have with you.

God seeks a love relationship with you. He is knocking. Will you invite Him in? Will you enjoy fellowship with Him? Will you love Him? Will you permit Him to live with you? You may have already entered a saving relationship with Jesus Christ. For the remainder of this study, we will assume that you have done so. If you have not, find a pastor or a Christian friend to help you surrender your life to Christ as your Savior and Lord. This love relationship is the point at which effective prayer begins.

Revelation 3:20
"Listen! I stand at the door and knock. If anyone hears My voice and opens the door, I will come in to him and have dinner with him, and he with Me."

 Pause and thank God for inviting you into a love relationship with Him. Ask Him to deepen your experience of His presence in prayer.

John 14:23
"If anyone loves Me, he will keep My word. My Father will love him, and We will come to him and make Our home with him."

In John 15:7 Jesus makes a special promise to those who abide in Him: "If you remain in Me and My words remain in you, ask whatever you want and it will be done for you." If you have a love relationship with Him and His words (teachings and commands) have become a part of your life, Jesus promises to respond to your prayers. The need for His words to remain in you is an important reason you are encouraged to memorize a Scripture passage each week. Hide God's words in your mind and heart.

This love relationship with God is the point at which effective prayer begins.

2) Cut out the Scripture-memory cards at the back of your book and begin memorizing Matthew 21:22. Read it several times. Meditate

on its meaning for you. Repeat it aloud phrase by phrase until you can say it without looking. Review it each week during our study.

Jesus also makes a special prayer promise to those who pray together in His name: "If two of you on earth agree about any matter that you pray for, it will be done for you by My Father in heaven. For where two or three are gathered together in My name, I am there among them" (Matthew 18:19-20). In this passage Jesus makes two promises for united prayer in which two or more pray together in agreement:
1. God gives greater authority to united prayer.
2. God is present where two or more gather in His name.

This course is designed to help you experience these two promises. We want you to learn the great authority God has granted to believers when they pray together in agreement. Many people are not seeing answers to prayer. This says more about their praying than it does about God. He has not changed. He still answers prayer. We will help you learn to pray more effectively as you follow biblical patterns for prayer.

This course is also designed to help you pray with other believers. God promises that those who gather to pray in His name experience a greater dimension of His presence. We reflect the unity within the Trinity when we pray together in agreement with the Lord.

③ **Have you made plans to pray with other believers as you study *Pray in Faith*?** ○ Yes ○ No **If yes, with whom will you pray?**

_____

_____

If you have not made plans to pray with others, begin to do so now. See page 110 for suggestions.

 Each day you will close your study time with a prayer time. Feel free to expand your prayer time as long as you please. Learning to pray comes with experience and practice. Today talk to the Lord about your love relationship with Him. Share with Him your desires for this study. Ask Him to teach you to be a person of prayer. Ask Him to make your prayer group people of prayer.

> Those who gather to pray in His name experience a greater dimension of His presence. We reflect the unity within the Trinity.

Day 2 • Responding and Asking Prayers

Today's Prayer Promise

"Call to Me and I will answer you and tell you great and wondrous things you do not know" (Jeremiah 33:3).

Prayer does not begin with you. God takes the initiative; He begins the relationship. God comes to you and gives you the desire to spend time with Him in prayer: "It is God who is working in you, enabling you both to will and to act for His good purpose" (Philippians 2:13).

① **Where does prayer begin?**
  ○ a. Prayer begins with me. I am the one who chooses to pray.
  ○ b. Prayer begins with God. He causes me to want to pray.

Prayer always begins with God. Even though you may think you decide to pray, God is the One who gives you the desire. Whenever you have the desire to pray, God is extending a personal invitation for you to spend time with Him. In prayer God wants you to identify with Him in two ways:
1. God wants you to identify with Him by becoming like His perfect Son, Jesus Christ.
2. God also wants you to identify with His purposes. He wants you to cooperate in accomplishing His purposes by asking for things that will advance His kingdom (His rule). You identify with Him by working with Him in prayer.

Two Purposes in Prayer

1. To identify with God by becoming like Him
2. To identify with God by working with Him in prayer

God gave you different kinds of prayer to accomplish these two patterns of identification with Him. During our study we will learn about six kinds of prayer, which fall into two groups. Some prayer is responding to God. In *responding prayers* you respond to God as a Person. You are learning to be a certain kind of person—a person like God Himself. **Being** is the important emphasis. As you talk to Him, God leads you to know Him and His ways so that you can become like Him.

② **What is one group of prayers?**
  R_____ prayers

Responding Prayers

1. Confession
2. Praise
3. Worship
4. Thanksgiving

Responding prayers include confession, praise, worship, and thanksgiving. These are listed for you in the chart on page 91. The other group of prayers is asking prayers. In *asking prayers* you are concerned with God's work. **Doing** is the important emphasis. As God leads your asking, you become involved with Him in His work.

③ Besides responding prayers, what is another group of prayers?

A _____ prayers

Asking prayers include prayers of petition, in which you pray for yourself and God's work in your life. Asking prayers also include intercession, in which you pray for God's work in and through others.

④ **Drawing lines across the columns, match the group of prayers on the left with the purpose of identification with God on the right.**

Responding prayers   Participating in God's work

Asking prayers   Becoming like God

In responding prayers you identify with God by becoming like Him. For instance, God reveals His holiness to you by revealing His purity. Then you may see impurities in your life. You respond to God's holiness by confessing and turning away from your impurities. Through this responding prayer you become more like God.

⑤ **Write below the four kinds of responding prayers. If you need help, review the chart in the Discipleship Helps on page 91.**

C_____ is responding to God's holiness.

P_____ is responding to God's attributes.

W_____ is responding to God's glory.

T_____ is responding to God's riches.

In asking prayers you identify with God by participating with Him in His work. For instance, God as your Master may lead you to ask Him for adults to work with youth in your church. God answers your prayer by giving a young couple a desire to work with youth. When they respond, you know God accomplished His purposes in answer to prayer. Through this asking prayer you worked together with God.

⑥ **Using the chart on page 91, write the two kinds of asking prayers.**

P_____ is asking that is led by your Heavenly Father.

I_____ is asking that is led by your Master.

 Pray, asking God to help you become more like Him. Agree to allow God to involve you in His work through prayer.

Asking Prayers
1. Petition
2. Intercession

In responding prayers you identify with God by becoming like Him.

In asking prayers you identify with God by participating with Him in His work.

Day 3 • Four Kinds of Responding Prayers

Today's Prayer Promise
"Sacrifice a thank offering to God, and pay your vows to the Most High. Call on Me in a day of trouble; I will rescue you, and you will honor Me" (Psalm 50:14-15).

✳ *holiness:* separate, morally pure, righteous, free from sin

✳ *confession:* agreeing with the truth, acknowledging your sin to God

Confession
"Be gracious to me, God, according to Your faithful love; according to Your abundant compassion, blot out my rebellion. Wash away my guilt, and cleanse me from my sin. For I am conscious of my rebellion, and my sin is always before me. Against You—You alone—I have sinned and done this evil in Your sight. So You are right when You pass sentence; You are blameless when You judge. God, create a clean heart for me and renew a steadfast spirit within me. Restore the joy of Your salvation to me, and give me a willing spirit" (Psalm 51:1-4,10,12).

God wants you, as His child, to identify with Him by becoming like Him. God reveals Himself and His ways to you so that you can become like Him. In a love relationship with you, God reveals what He is like. As you respond to Him in that relationship, you can become more like Him.

1. **Which of the following is the purpose of responding prayers?**
   ○ a. I identify with God by working with Him in His kingdom.
   ○ b. I identify with God by becoming like Him.

CONFESSION: RESPONDING TO GOD'S HOLINESS
By responding to God in prayer, you become more like Him (b). One trait God reveals about Himself is His ***holiness****. He is separate, pure, and righteous. God reveals that He is holy and that He wants you to be holy like Him. He wants you to be pure and set apart for His purposes. But sometimes you are not holy. You sin. When you sin, you do not lose your holiness, but you interrupt the process of growing in holiness, or sanctification. Confession restores the process of gradual sanctification. Because sin is offensive to God, it hinders your intimate fellowship with Him. The Holy Spirit convicts you of the sin, and you can use a prayer of confession to restore the fellowship. ***Confession**** is saying the same thing God says, or agreeing with God. You agree with God about the nature of your sin. Because you love Him, you want to return to Him (repent) and become more like Him. Confession is responding to God's holiness.

2. **Fill in the blanks below with the first kind of responding prayer and the aspect of God to which you are responding. Then read an example in the left margin.**
   C _____ is responding to God's h _____.

PRAISE: RESPONDING TO GOD'S ATTRIBUTES
God reveals His attributes or character traits because He wants you to become like Him. As you grow in your knowledge of God, especially through Bible study, you will know His attributes. When you know what God is like, you want to praise Him. Praise lifts up or focuses on God's attributes. Praise exalts God in His divinity—because of what He is like. Praise is responding to God's attributes.

(3) What is a second kind of responding prayer, and to which aspects of God are you responding? Fill in the blanks and read an example in the right margin.

P _____ is responding to God's a _____ .

WORSHIP: RESPONDING TO GOD'S GLORY

When God acts to reveal Himself, He displays His glory. Glory is the evidence of God's attributes (what He is like). God reveals His glory through His mighty acts. All creation reveals God's glory. When you see God's glory, you love Him. Worship is responding to God's glory. Worship is adoring, loving, and honoring God. Worship is much more personal and intimate than praise. Worship is the expression of your love, adoration, reverence, and honor for God.

(4) In addition to confession and praise, what is a third kind of responding prayer, and to which aspect of God are you responding? Fill in the blanks and read an example in the right margin.

W _____ is responding to God's g_____ .

THANKSGIVING: RESPONDING TO GOD'S RICHES

God reveals His riches—both physical and spiritual. God is the Giver of every perfect gift. He wants you to experience the abundant life He has to give you. Thanksgiving is responding to and participating in God's riches. Ephesians 5:20 tells you to thank God in everything. Thanksgiving is not just an event or a statement. It is an attitude. God wants you to have an attitude of gratitude.

(5) In addition to confession, praise, and worship, what is a forth kind of responding prayer, and to which aspects of God are you responding? Fill in the blanks and read an example in the right margin.

T _____ is responding to God's r_____ .

 Review the four kinds of responding prayers. Then spend a few minutes praying and responding to evidences of God's holiness, attributes, glory, and riches with prayers of confession, praise, worship, and thanksgiving.

Praise
"Yahweh is great and is highly praised; His greatness is unsearchable. One generation will declare Your works to the next and will proclaim Your mighty acts. I will speak of Your glorious splendor and Your wonderful works. They will proclaim the power of Your awe-inspiring works, and I will declare Your greatness. They will give a testimony of Your great goodness and will joyfully sing of Your righteousness" (Psalm 145: 3-7).

Worship
"As a deer longs for streams of water, so I long for You, God. I thirst for God, the living God" (Psalm 42:1-2).

Thanksgiving
"Give thanks to the LORD, for He is good. His love is eternal. He spread the land on the waters. His love is eternal. He remembered us in our humiliation His love is eternal. and rescued us from our foes. His love is eternal. Give thanks to the God of heaven! His love is eternal" (Psalm 136:1,6,23-24,26).

Day 4 • Two Kinds of Asking Prayers

1. To review yesterday's lesson, list the four kinds of responding prayers. Check your answers on page 91.

_____ is responding to God's holiness.

_____ is responding to God's attributes.

_____ is responding to God's glory.

_____ is responding to God's riches.

In responding prayers you respond to the Person of God or to the aspects of who He is (holiness, attributes, glory, riches). The other group of prayers is asking prayers, emphasized in Jesus' greatest teaching sessions:

> "Keep asking, and it will be given to you. Keep searching, and you will find. Keep knocking, and the door will be opened to you" (Matthew 7:7).

> "If you ask Me anything in My name, I will do it" (John 14:14).

> "If you remain in Me and My words remain in you, ask whatever you want and it will be done for you" (John 15:7).

> "Until now you have asked for nothing in My name. Ask and you will receive, that your joy may be complete" (John 16:24).

The Bible teaches two kinds of asking prayers: petition and intercession. Asking prayers are not direct responses to the *Person* of God. As God takes the lead in the asking prayers, you follow His lead and participate with Him in His *work*. The great purpose in asking prayers is for you to identify with His purposes. God is interested in your asking prayers. God wants you to cooperate in accomplishing His purposes by asking for things that will advance His kingdom (His rule).

2. Which of the following is the purpose of asking prayers?
   ○ a. I identify with God by working with Him in His kingdom.
   ○ b. I identify with God by becoming like Him.

Today's Prayer Promise

"This is the confidence we have before Him: whenever we ask anything according to His will, He hears us. And if we know that He hears whatever we ask, we know that we have what we have asked Him for" (1 John 5:14-15).

Individual Petition

(David's prayer for himself)
"LORD, I turn my hope to You. My God, I trust in You. Do not let me be disgraced; do not let my enemies gloat over me. Make Your ways known to me, LORD; teach me Your paths. Guide me in Your truth and teach me, for You are the God of my salvation; I wait for You all day long" (Psalm 25:1-2,4-5).

Through asking prayers God brings about His purposes in your life and in the lives of others for whom you pray by involving you in His work (a). Let's overview the two kinds of asking prayers.

PETITION: ASKING LED BY YOUR HEAVENLY FATHER

Petition is asking for yourself, your family, your church, or your group. God reveals Himself as a Father. When you are redeemed, you are adopted into His family. As His child, you address your requests to your Heavenly Father.

God's purpose in encouraging your petition is to mold you into a certain kind of person—someone who reflects the life and character of His Son Jesus. Because your personal petition should be directed by your Heavenly Father, through this kind of prayer you become more like the person God wants you to be as He accomplishes His purposes in your life.

③ **What is one kind of asking prayer? P** _____
Who leads your petitions? My _____

④ **Read in the left and right margins examples of individual and group petition. Underline the requests made of God. One is underlined for you.**

INTERCESSION: ASKING LED BY YOUR MASTER

God reveals Himself as Master and Ruler. God is at work in His world, and He has chosen to do His work through people. When God gets ready to do something, He calls a person to intercession, which is asking for someone else. Your Master leads your intercession for others. Through intercession you work with God as His servant. Intercession is an important method God uses to accomplish His will among people.

⑤ **What is the second kind of asking prayer? I** _____
Who leads your intercession? My _____

⑥ **In the right margin, read the example of intercession. Underline the requests made of God on behalf of others. One is underlined for you.**

 Pause to pray, using Paul's requests in Ephesians 3:16-19 (in the right margin). First pray these requests for yourself. Then pray these requests for your church or prayer group.

Group Petition

(The early church's prayer for itself) "Master, You are the One who made the heaven, the earth, and the sea, and everything in them. And now, Lord, consider their threats, and grant that Your slaves may speak Your message with complete boldness, while You stretch out Your hand for healing, signs, and wonders to be performed through the name of Your holy Servant Jesus" (Acts 4:24,29-30).

Intercession

(Paul's prayer for the Ephesians) "I pray that He may grant you, according to the riches of His glory, to <u>be strengthened with power</u> through His Spirit in the inner man, and that the Messiah may dwell in your hearts through faith. I pray that you, being rooted and firmly established in love, may be able to comprehend with all the saints what is the breadth and width, height and depth, and to know the Messiah's love that surpasses knowledge, so you may be filled with all the fullness of God" (Ephesians 3:16-19).

Day 5 • Praying with Others

Today's Prayer Promise
"Thus saith the high and lofty One that inhabiteth eternity, whose name is Holy; I dwell in the high and holy place, with him also that is of a contrite and humble spirit, to revive the spirit of the humble, and to revive the heart of the contrite ones'" (Isaiah 57:15, KJV).

Seek to develop the character of one with whom God dwells. He brings the humble and contrite into His presence.

We hope you have been paying attention to the prayer promise at the beginning of each day. You may want to write the most meaningful promises on index cards and memorize them.

1. **Read today's prayer promise and complete the following activities.**
   a. Circle some of the ways God is described in this verse.
   b. What are two places in which God chooses to dwell? Number them.
   c. What are two reasons God chooses to dwell with those who are humble and contrite? Underline them.

2. **Which set of the following characteristics best describes you?**
   ○ a. Humble and contrite
   ○ b. Proud, arrogant, remorseless

If you are interested in experiencing God's presence, seek to develop the character of one with whom God dwells. He brings the humble and contrite into His presence. He does not dwell with the proud and arrogant.

Day 5 of each week in this study focuses on praying together. Often we are so familiar with praying alone that we pray with others the same way we do by ourselves. Does the following describe prayer meetings you have attended?
1. Intercessor 1 prays through his mental list while other group members check off these subjects on their mental lists.
2. Intercessor 2 prays through the remaining items on her mental list while other group members check off items on their mental lists.
3. Intercessor 3 has little left on his list about which to pray.
4. Intercessor 4, feeling that almost everything has been covered, closes the prayer time.

Not every group prayer time is like that. However, we miss some exciting dimensions of praying together if we only pray through long mental lists. We suggest that you and your prayer group consider some guidelines for praying together more effectively.

3. **Read "Suggestions for Praying Together" on page 110. In each suggestion underline a word or a phrase to help you remember it.**

(4) **Now review the words or phrases. Circle the numbers beside the three suggestions you believe will be most helpful for your prayer group to practice.**

At least once each week we will discuss ways your prayer group can pray together more effectively. Today we will examine two suggestions.

ACKNOWLEDGE GOD'S PRESENCE AND PARTICIPATION

God promised His presence where two or more are gathered in His name (see Matthew 18:20). He is also actively involved when you pray together. Both the Holy Spirit and Jesus intercede for and with you (see Romans 8:26-27,34; Hebrews 7:25). When you meet with a group to pray, remember that God is present. Think of your prayer time as a conversation among your group members and God. Speak to Him. Listen to what God may say to you as He guides your group to Scriptures and as He guides your prayers. You may speak to one another as well as share prayer concerns during your prayer.

(5) **When your group gathers to pray, who should be the focus of attention?**
   ○ a. I should be the focus of attention. I am important.
   ○ b. Our group leader should be the focus. We need her guidance.
   ○ c. God must be the focus. He is the most important One present.

Because prayer is a conversation among your group members and God, He should be the focus of your time together (c).

PREPARE YOURSELVES THROUGH CONFESSION

If you were entering the court of a king or a queen, you would want to be prepared. You would want to dress and act correctly. In a similar way, your group will want to prepare for entering the throne room of heaven. Jesus has made a way for your cleansing as you confess and turn from your sin (see 1 John 1:9). In your prayer-group meeting take time for individuals to prepare themselves in silent prayer. You may also want to take time to "confess your sins to one another and pray for one another" (James 5:16).

 Read the Discipleship Help on confession (pp. 92–93). Spend time in prayers of confession. Ask God to cleanse you thoroughly. Pray for your prayer-group members as they also prepare for your time together in prayer this week.

Matthew 18:
"Where two or th[...]
ered together in My n[...]
I am there among them."

Romans 8:26-27,34
"The Spirit also joins to help in our weakness, because we do not know what to pray for as we should, but the Spirit Himself intercedes for us with unspoken groanings. And He who searches the hearts knows the Spirit's mind-set, because He intercedes for the saints according to the will of God. Who is the one who condemns? Christ Jesus is the One who died, but even more, has been raised; He also is at the right hand of God and intercedes for us."

Hebrews 7:25
"He [Christ] is always able to save those who come to God through Him, since He always lives to intercede for them."

1 John 1:9
"If we confess our sins, He is faithful and righteous to forgive us our sins and to cleanse us from all unrighteousness."

20

...e are gath-
...me,

Week 2
Developing Your Prayer Life

"If two of you on earth agree about
any matter that you pray for, it will
be done for you by My Father in heaven"
Matthew 18:19

Developing Your Prayer Life

OVERVIEW OF WEEK 2
Day 1: Reasons to Pray
Day 2: Daily Prayer
Day 3: Tools to Help You Pray
Day 4: The Bible and Prayer
Day 5: Being a House of Prayer

VERSE TO MEMORIZE
"If two of you on earth agree about any matter that you pray for, it will be done for you by My Father in heaven" (Matthew 18:19).

DISCIPLESHIP HELPS FOR WEEK 2
"Prayers of Praise" (pp. 94–95)

PREVIEW OF WEEK 2
When you are related to your Heavenly Father by adoption, prayer is a natural part of the relationship. You talk to Him, and He talks to you. This relationship can be neglected or developed. This week we want to help you develop your personal prayer relationship with your Heavenly Father. This week you will—
• identify 10 reasons to pray;
• learn how prayer can and should be a constant, natural part of your day;
• use some practical tools to enrich your personal prayer life;
• learn ways to use the Bible in your prayers;
• understand the importance of your church's being a house of prayer.

Day 1 • Reasons to Pray

Prayer is a relationship with your Heavenly Father. He created you for a love relationship with Himself. If you love someone, you want to spend time with him or her. If you love God, you want to spend time with Him. That conscious time you spend in God's presence is what we call prayer. One of the best reasons to pray is to spend time with the One you love.

1 What is one of the best reasons to pray?

_____

Spending time with the One you love is a great reason to pray. Last week you studied two purposes of prayer. God wants you to identify with Him by becoming like Him and by working together with Him.

2 Read John 15:16; Romans 8:29; and 2 Corinthians 3:18 in the margin. Match the Scripture references below with the reasons to pray by writing a letter beside each reference.

___ John 15:16   a. To become like God (Jesus)
___ Romans 8:29   b. To work together with God
___ 2 Corinthians 3:18

3 Read the following verses and underline other reasons to pray. We've underlined one for you.

Matthew 26:40-41 • "Couldn't you stay awake with Me one hour? Stay awake and pray, <u>so that you won't enter into temptation</u>."

Luke 18:13-14 • "The tax collector, standing far off, would not even raise his eyes to heaven but kept striking his chest and saying, 'God, turn Your wrath from me—a sinner!' I tell you, this one went down to his house justified."

John 16:24 • "Ask and you will receive, that your joy may be complete."

Romans 8:26-27 • "We do not know what to pray for as we should, but the Spirit Himself intercedes for us … according to the will of God."

Scripture-Memory Verse

"If two of you on earth agree about any matter that you pray for, it will be done for you by My Father in heaven" (Matthew 18:19).

John 15:16

"You did not choose Me, but I chose you. I appointed you that you should go out and produce fruit and that your fruit should remain, so that whatever you ask the Father in My name, He will give you."

Romans 8:29

"Those He foreknew He also predestined to be conformed to the image of His Son."

2 Corinthians 3:18

"We all, with unveiled faces, are reflecting the glory of the Lord and are being transformed into the same image from glory to glory; this is from the Lord who is the Spirit."

#2 answers:
a–John 15:16;
b–Romans 8:29; 2 Corinthians 3:18

Hebrews 4:16 • "Let us approach the throne of grace with boldness, so that we may receive mercy and find grace to help us at the proper time."

Hebrews 13:15 • "Let us continually offer up to God a sacrifice of praise."

More reasons to pray include: to gain strength to resist temptation (Matthew 26:40-41), to be justified (made right) with God (Luke 18:13-14), to experience fullness of joy (John 16:24), to know God's will (Romans 8:26-27), to find mercy and grace (Hebrews 4:16), and to offer sacrifices to God (Hebrews 13:15).

Two more reasons to pray are to learn authority and to release God's power. In the beginning God granted authority and dominion to Adam. When Adam sinned and fell, he lost the authority God intended for all humanity. But Jesus' sinless life and sacrificial death made it possible for us to recover all Adam lost. As believers, we are now seated with Christ and are joint heirs with Him. God is in the process of restoring our authority by training us to use our authority properly. In eternity we will exercise that authority by reigning with Christ (see Revelation 5:10).

Because prayer is God's training ground, continual prayer instills authority in us. We learn proper authority when we pray rightly and God answers. We learn wrong uses of authority when we pray incorrectly and God refuses our request.

Authority controls power. When you learn to use authority properly, you release God's power in answer to prayer. Exercising your authority in prayer releases God's power.

(4) **What are two more reasons to pray?**

To learn _____

To release God's _____

 Review in the margin the list of reasons to pray. Ask the Lord which reason you need to emphasize most in your life today. Circle it and spend a few minutes in prayer for that reason.

Revelation 5:10
"You made them a kingdom and priests to our God, and they will reign on the earth."

10 Reasons to Pray
1. To spend time with God— the One you love
2. To identify with God by becoming like Him
3. To identify with God by working together with Him
4. To gain strength to resist temptation
5. To be made right with God
6. To find forgiveness, mercy, and grace
7. To learn God's will
8. To offer sacrifices to God
9. To learn authority
10. To release God's power

Day 2 • Daily Prayer

Today's Prayer Promise

"You did not choose Me, but I chose you. I appointed you that you should go out and produce fruit and that your fruit should remain, so that whatever you ask the Father in My name, He will give you" (John 15:16).

1 Thessalonians 5:17

"Pray constantly."

Hebrews 13:15

"Through Him [Jesus] let us continually offer up to God a sacrifice of praise."

You can always be in a spirit of prayer because you have an uninterrupted relationship with God.

Because prayer is a relationship with God, prayer can actually be continual (see 1 Thessalonians 5:17; Hebrews 13:15). You need to live your life in such an attitude that you can talk to God anytime. You always need to listen so that He can speak to you at any time. God is always present with you as a believer. Therefore, you can pray continually.

"Search for the LORD and for His strength;
seek His face always" (1 Chronicles 16:11).

"He [Jesus] then told them a parable on the need for them to pray always and not become discouraged" (Luke 18:1).

"With every prayer and request, pray at all times in the Spirit, and stay alert in this, with all perseverance and intercession for all the saints" (Ephesians 6:18).

1. **Based on these verses, how often should a believer pray during a day?**
   ○ a. Ten minutes in the morning and a blessing at each meal
   ○ b. Three times a day, 15 minutes each time
   ○ c. One hour a day
   ○ d. Always, continually

Did you check (d) *Always, continually?* Does that seem impossible? It is … if you see prayer as a religious activity that you perform at certain times each day. God created you for a relationship with Him. He is always present and can speak to you anytime. You can pray anytime. You can always be in a spirit of prayer because you have an uninterrupted relationship with God.

Try to envision a day in which you pray continually. You awake in the morning and thank God for a new day. You take time to be alone with Him. You read a passage from your Bible, through which God speaks to you. You spend time in confession, praise, worship, and thanksgiving. You talk to God about your life, what you need, and what He wants you to be. You pray for others and seek God's work in them and the circumstances they face. After you say, "Amen," are you finished praying for today? No, you shouldn't be.

You continue to listen to God and pray as you shower. You thank Him for your food and His blessings as you eat breakfast. You pray with and for your children before they leave for school. On your way to work, you pray for God's involvement in your work, for problems, for relationships, and for witnessing opportunities. While you are praying, your attention is captured by the beauty of a tree's leaves that are turning colors, and you worship God for the beauty of the earth and for His grandeur in creating it. A problem arises at work, and you whisper a prayer to your Master in heaven for guidance. He guides you to resolve the problem, and you drop to your knees in your office to thank Him. A coworker mentions a family problem, and you pray with her. You continue to commune with God throughout the day until bedtime, when you thank Him for the blessings of the day.

② Think about a typical day. When are natural times to approach your Heavenly Father in prayers of confession, praise, worship, thanksgiving, petition, and intercession? List at least five times.

_____

_____

③ Spend today or tomorrow in an attitude of prayer all day, recognizing that God is always present. Be alert to times and ways you can pray privately as well as with others.

TIMES AND PLACES TO PRAY

You can pray anytime and anywhere. Jesus prayed at different times and in a wide variety of places. (Read the Scriptures under Jesus' Example in the margin.) Sometimes you can pray aloud, and sometimes you must pray silently. No one can prevent you from praying, even in a place where public prayer is not permitted, because God is always present with you.

Many believers begin the day with a quiet time with God in prayer. Daniel prayed three times a day (see Daniel 6:10 in the margin). Try to spend concentrated time in prayer, whether morning, noon, or evening. For these regular times of private prayer, find a place where you can be alone with God.

↕ Take a few moments to pray about your personal prayer life. Ask God to direct you to make the adjustments necessary to develop a meaningful lifestyle of prayer.

Jesus' Example

"Very early in the morning, while it was still dark, He got up, went out, and made His way to a deserted place. And He was praying there" (Mark 1:35).

"After He said good-bye to them, He went away to the mountain to pray. When evening came, … He was alone on the land" (Mark 6:46-47).

"He [Jesus] often withdrew to deserted places and prayed" (Luke 5:16).

"He [Jesus] went out to the mountain to pray and spent all night in prayer to God" (Luke 6:12).

Daniel 6:10

"When Daniel learned that the document [a law against prayer] had been signed, he went into his house. The windows in its upper room opened toward Jerusalem, and three times a day he got down on his knees, prayed, and gave thanks to his God, just as he had done before."

Day 3 • Tools to Help You Pray

Today's Prayer Promise
"Everything is possible to the one who believes" (Mark 9:23).

Ecclesiastes 5:2
"Do not be hasty to speak, and do not be impulsive to make a speech before God."

Prayers of Confession (p. 92)
You are my Father;
I am Your child.

Prayers of Praise (p. 94)
"My lips will glorify You because Your faithful love is better than life" (Psalm 63:3).

Prayers of Worship (p. 96)
"The Lamb who was slaughtered is worthy to receive power and riches and wisdom and strength and honor and glory and blessing!" (Revelation 5:12).

You may have some simple yet practical questions about prayer. The remaining lessons this week will give you suggestions for developing your personal prayer life. Today we will share with you some tools we have used that may help in your personal prayer life.

Organizing your thoughts in prayer is one way to show reverence for God (see Ecclesiastes 5:2). A prayer list provides reminders for many of the areas for which you need to pray. Keep a list in your Bible, organize a notebook, or use a computer file to guide your praying. We've developed the Discipleship Helps section to serve as your prayer journal for the next few weeks.

1 Take a few minutes to flip through the Discipleship Helps on pages 91–110 to see the tools we've prepared for you to use.

2 Read the following descriptions of prayer lists. In the margins we've given you a sample for each list. After you read about a list, turn to the appropriate page at the back of this book and list persons, concerns, topics, and requests that you want to include in your own prayer times.

Confession, praise, worship, and thanksgiving lists. You may want to keep separate lists to use daily in your responding prayers. On these lists you might record attributes of God, items for which you are thankful, truths you want to confess, and so forth.

Daily requests. Keep a list of persons and subjects you pray for daily. Include members of your family, your pastor, close friends, those in authority over you, and continuing concerns you want to pray for daily.

Daily temporary requests. Keep a daily temporary list of persons and concerns that change from time to time. Include special projects you are working on, sick friends, and other temporary requests.

Weekly requests. Each day of the week make a separate list of concerns you pray for on the same day each week. These weekly lists could include friends, church concerns, upcoming events, governments, elected officials, missionaries, lost people who need Christ, and other less frequent requests.

Monthly requests. For each day of the month make a list that includes items of importance or concern but somewhat removed from your immediate situation. Pray for the items you have listed for each day of the month. These might include praying for a different country each day or relatives.

Scriptures. For many items on your lists you may want to write appropriate Scriptures. For example, write Scriptures that apply to a Christian spouse as you pray for your spouse. Choose other Scriptures that guide your prayers for your pastor, missionaries, Christian leaders, and others.

Using your lists. Do not follow your lists so rigorously that the practice becomes legalistic, routine, or ritualistic. Prayer must be personal and intimate. Use your lists as general guides to—
• prevent your praying from focusing exclusively on yourself;
• aid your memory so that you do not forget special concerns;
• assign an order of importance to your requests if time is limited.

Also plan free periods of prayer in which you joyfully follow the Holy Spirit's leading in many matters, including concerns, praise, and thanksgiving. Be sensitive to ways your Father guides you to pray and listen for direction from your Master. During these times God may remind you of a person or a need that is not on your lists. These occasions can become special times of intercession. You may even want to set aside one day each week for "free prayer."

OTHER PRAYER TOOLS

All you need for prayer is the Lord's presence. However, you can use certain tools to enrich your prayer time. You may want to use a hymnal in prayer, for many hymn texts are prayers to God. You can pray a song or sing a hymn to the Lord.

Many people like to use journals for writing their prayers to the Lord. Writing your prayers can help you focus on your requests and can remind you of your prayer when the answer comes. You may also want to use books on prayer, biographies of great people of prayer, maps, pictures, or other reminders for prayer.

As you pray to close this lesson, use some of the items you included on your lists as subjects for your prayers. You may want to take some extra time to expand your prayer lists.

Prayers of Thanksgiving (p. 98)
Salvation,
privilege to serve,
good health

Daily Requests (p. 104)
Laverne (my wife)

Daily Temporary Requests (p. 104)
A volunteer to lead our church's prayer ministry

Weekly Requests (p. 105)
Monday: Terry and Sue, missionaries in Chile

Monthly Requests (p. 108)
15th: Calvary Church—unity
21st: Ghana, Honduras, Russia, Vietnam

Day 4 • The Bible and Prayer

Today's Prayer Promise
"Whoever keeps His word, truly in him the love of God is perfected. This is how we know we are in Him: the one who says he remains in Him should walk just as He walked" (1 John 2:5-6).

Years ago I (T. W.) reached a point in my morning devotions at which I gave large blocks of time to prayer and only a few minutes to Bible study. Then I heard E. F. Hallock, a great preacher, say that we should not have to choose between time in the Bible and time in prayer. If a choice has to be made, it is more important that God speak to the individual than that a person speak to God. That statement reformed my prayer life. I began reading, studying, memorizing, and meditating on Scriptures more frequently. I found myself and my prayers increasingly being shaped by the words of Scripture that had become lodged in my subconscious.

Bible reading and study do not have to be separate activities from prayer. The Bible is another way God speaks. Therefore, prayer and Bible reading should be practiced together. By praying the words of the Bible, you learn to think God's thoughts. Listen to what God may want to say to you as you read and study your Bible. Let the Scriptures point you to your love relationship with God.

John 5:39-40
"You pore over the Scriptures because you think you have eternal life in them, yet they testify about Me. And you are not willing to come to Me that you may have life."

1. **Read John 5:39-40 in the margin. Where should a study of the Scriptures lead you?**
   ○ a. I find eternal life in a study of the Scriptures.
   ○ b. The Scriptures lead me to a knowledge of good literature.
   ○ c. The Scriptures point me to a long list of do's and don'ts.
   ○ d. The Scriptures point me to a living relationship with Jesus.

Jesus was speaking to the Jewish leaders (probably the Pharisees) in John 5:39-40. They knew studying the Scriptures was important. Yet they had so emphasized and prided themselves in gaining knowledge that they had missed the whole purpose—a living relationship with God through His Son, Jesus Christ. You too need to emphasize studying, reading, memorizing, and meditating on Scriptures. But don't place your focus on knowledge alone. Always look through the Scriptures to God. The Scriptures will lead you to Jesus, and He gives you life. He is your life!

Memorizing and meditating on (or thinking about) Scriptures are also valuable activities for your devotional life.

2. Read Joshua 1:8; Psalm 119:11,105 in the right margin.
   a. When should you meditate on Scriptures?

   _____

   b. What is one reason for memorizing God's Word?

   _____

   c. What is a practical way God's Word can help you?

   _____

The Bible is a practical guide for living. It shows you God's will and God's ways. One reason for memorizing God's Word is so that you will not sin against God. When you know what God says about an activity or a relationship, you can obey what He commands. Meditating on the Scriptures you have memorized can also help you observe and do what God says. These Scriptures should be the subject of your thinking day and night. Scriptures are very valuable in shaping and guiding your prayer life.

3. Read in the margin some ways to use Scriptures in prayer. Draw a star beside one that you have or would like to use.

As you use Scriptures in prayer, ask the Holy Spirit to guide you in applying them to particular situations.

4. Who has the right to decide which promises or Scriptures apply to situations for which you are praying?
   ○ a. I do. If I find a Scripture I like, I can claim it as a promise and pressure God to do what I want.
   ○ b. The Holy Spirit does. Only He knows God's mind and will. When He gives me a Scripture, I can depend on God to keep His Word.

The Holy Spirit will guide you in using Scriptures to pray. Trust Him to help you when you don't know what to pray. He is ready to help.

↕ Close today's lesson by praying through Psalm 139 in your Bible. Observe that the Scriptures can be a wonderful aid in prayer.

Joshua 1:8
"This book of instruction must not depart from your mouth; you are to recite it day and night, so that you may carefully observe every-thing written in it. For then you will prosper and succeed in whatever you do."

Psalm 119:11
"I have treasured Your word in my heart so that I may not sin against You."

Psalm 119:105
"Your word is a lamp for my feet and a light on my path."

Ways to Use Scriptures in Prayer
1. Quote a promise as assur-ance of an answer.
2. Quote a fulfilled promise as a reason for praise.
3. Apply Bible verses to a current situation.
4. Use Bible verses as a prayer or praise.
5. Use Bible phrases in a prayer.

Ask the Holy Spirit to guide you in applying Scriptures to particular situations.

Day 5 • Being a House of Prayer

Today's Prayer Promise

"Even before they call, I will answer; while they are still speaking, I will hear" (Isaiah 65:24).

The Model Prayer

"You should pray like this: Our Father in heaven, Your name be honored as holy. Your kingdom come. Your will be done on earth as it is in heaven. Give us today our daily bread. And forgive us our debts, as we also have forgiven our debtors. And do not bring us into temptation, but deliver us from the evil one. For Yours is the kingdom and the power and the glory forever" (Matthew 6:9-13).

A church must be a house of prayer, or it may begin to oppose God and what He wants to accomplish.

Jesus taught His disciples to pray. Nearly all His teaching on prayer focused on corporate or group prayer, using words like *you* (plural), *our*, *we*, and *us*.

1. **Read the Model Prayer (Matthew 6:9-13) in the margin. Circle the words *you*, *we*, *our*, and *us*.**

Jesus began by saying, *"You* [plural] should pray like this: *Our* Father. ... Give *us*. ... Forgive *us*, ... as *we*. ... And do not bring *us* ..."* (Matthew 6:9-13, emphasis added). God intended for His people to pray together. He said, "My house will be called a house of prayer for all nations" (Isaiah 56:7).

God wanted His house to be a house of prayer. In Luke 19 Jesus wept over Jerusalem because the people had refused to accept Him—the One who could have brought them peace. Then He made His way to the temple. There Jesus drove out of the temple those who were buying and selling animals. "He said, 'It is written, My house will be a house of prayer, but you have made it a den of thieves!'" (v. 46). Because God's people were no longer a house of prayer, they sought to destroy Jesus when He came to them. A church must be a house of prayer, or it may begin to oppose God and what He wants to accomplish.

2. **If God evaluated your church, would He say that you are a house and people of prayer? Check the statement that best describes your church.**
   ○ Yes, prayer is our life. We devote extended times to prayer and can testify to many answers to prayer. Our people know how to pray effectively. Other people know us as a people of prayer.
   ○ No, we do not pray together often. Most of our prayers are brief and general. Usually, only one person prays. Our prayer meetings are poorly attended, and we seldom hear testimonies of answered prayer.
   ○ Other. Describe in the left margin.

Perhaps you could not check either of the first two statements because your church falls somewhere between these two extremes. If you had to check no, we have some good news for you. The very fact that you are studying this course and are learning to pray together with other believers indicates that God is at work! He may be preparing to take you and your church to a deeper level of united prayer than you have known.

③ Read in the margin Scriptures describing the prayer activities of the early church. Was the early church a house of prayer? ○ Yes ○ No

PRAYING IN UNITY

The early Christians were a group of united believers who prayed earnestly. The importance of the disciples' unity is seen repeatedly in Jesus' great prayer in John 17 (see vv. 11,21,23). Jesus wanted the disciples to be one, to be united with a single purpose and spirit. He wanted them to be united just as He and God the Father are united. When this kind of unity is expressed in the church, the world around will know and believe that Jesus was indeed sent from God. Is it possible that our inadequacies in reaching people for Christ are due in part to our lack of unity? Probably so.

Jesus promises Christians a special presence when they gather together to pray: "I assure you: If two of you on earth agree about any matter that you pray for, it will be done for you by My Father in heaven. For where two or three are gathered together in My name, I am there among them" (Matthew 18:19-20). Jesus desires that the church be unified and that it pray together. This is exactly what we see in the beginnings of the church. Both the unity and the praying of the church are conspicuous, along with the results of its unified praying. The most powerful form of prayer available to the body of Christ is united prayer. The greater unity you present to God when you pray together, the greater the authority God invests in your prayer.

We have been praying for united prayer in churches for years. Would you join us in praying that God will help your church become a house of prayer that is pleasing to Him and is powerful in prayer? If you will, pray now for that result.

SUGGESTIONS FOR PRAYING TOGETHER THIS WEEK

When you pray together, individuals have a tendency to pray about several topics at one time. Pay special attention during this session to pray about one subject at a time. Take turns praying about that subject. One person may pray about the circumstances. Another may pray for the persons involved. Another may pray for God's glory, purpose, or will. One may claim a scriptural promise or recall a biblical pattern that seems to apply. Let the Holy Spirit guide your prayer on a topic. Continue to pray about that subject as long as God seems to guide the praying.

The Early Church:

"All these were continually united in prayer" (Acts 1:14).

"They devoted themselves to the apostles' teaching, to fellowship, to the breaking of bread, and to prayers" (Acts 2:42).

"We [the apostles] will devote ourselves to prayer and to the preaching ministry" (Acts 6:3).

"Peter was kept in prison, but prayer was being made earnestly to God for him by the church" (Acts 12:5).

John 17:11,21,23

"Holy Father, protect them by Your name that You have given Me, so that they may be one as We are one. May they all be one, as You, Father, are in Me and I am in You. May they also be one in Us, so the world may believe You sent Me. I am in them and You are in Me. May they be made completely one, so the world may know You have sent Me and have loved them as You have loved Me."

Week 3
Responding Prayers

"Through Him [Jesus] let us continually offer
up to God a sacrifice of praise, that is,
the fruit of our lips that confess His name."

Hebrews 13:15

Responding Prayers

OVERVIEW OF WEEK 3
Day 1: Confession: Responding to God's Holiness
Day 2: Praise: Responding to God's Attributes
Day 3: Worship: Responding to God's Glory
Day 4: Thanksgiving: Responding to God's Riches
Day 5: Responding Together

VERSE TO MEMORIZE
"Through Him [Jesus] let us continually offer up to God a sacrifice of praise,
that is, the fruit of our lips that confess His name" (Hebrews 13:15).

DISCIPLESHIP HELPS FOR WEEK 3
"Prayers of Confession" (pp. 92–93)
"Prayers of Praise" (pp. 94–95)
"Prayers of Worship" (pp. 96–97)
"Prayers of Thanksgiving" (pp. 98–99)

PREVIEW OF WEEK 3
This week you will—
• identify aspects God has revealed about Himself: His holiness, His attributes,
  His glory, and His riches;
• learn how to respond in prayer to God's aspects;
• understand that the purpose of responding prayers is to help you become the person
  God has planned for you to be;
• become more like God as you begin to respond to Him in confession, praise, worship,
  and thanksgiving;
• study in detail the four types of responding prayers.
  —Confession: responding to God's holiness
  —Praise: responding to God's attributes
  —Worship: responding to God's glory
  —Thanksgiving: responding to God's riches

Day 1 • Confession: Responding to God's Holiness

Scripture-Memory Verse
"Through Him [Jesus] let us continually offer up to God a sacrifice of praise, that is, the fruit of our lips that confess His name" (Hebrews 13:15).

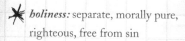

holiness: separate, morally pure, righteous, free from sin

God is holy. He is separate, pure, and righteous. God reveals His *holiness** because He wants you to be holy as He is holy: "It is written, 'Be holy, because I am holy'" (1 Peter 1:16). Yet we cannot be holy apart from God's work in us. When God revealed Himself to persons in biblical accounts, one of the first qualities they recognized was His holiness.

1. **Turn in your Bible and read Isaiah 6:1-7. Which of the following describes Isaiah's response to God's holiness?**
   ○ a. He realized his sin in the presence of God's holiness and cried out.
   ○ b. He was proud to be in God's presence and boasted of his own goodness and righteousness.

2. **How did God (through the seraphs) respond to Isaiah's cry?**
   ○ a. God killed Isaiah in His anger.
   ○ b. God cleansed and forgave Isaiah in His love and mercy.

Confronted with God's holiness, Isaiah cried out because of his sin (1–a). He agreed with what God already knew to be true. Isaiah had no reason to feel pride. God responded in love and mercy by taking away Isaiah's sin. Isaiah was cleansed and forgiven (2–b). Then he could be useful to God (see Isaiah 6:8-13).

CONFESSION

confession: agreeing with the truth, acknowledging your sin to God

The Greek word for *confess* means *speak the same thing* or *agree with.* In one way all prayer is agreeing with God. *Confession** is agreeing with the truth. When you sin, God feels sadness or grief. You tend to feel guilty because of your sin. Satan, as "the accuser of our brothers" (Revelation 12:10), reminds you of your sin so that you will feel guilty. Your guilt may cause you to run away or hide from God, as Adam and Eve did in the garden of Eden.

God is more interested in your agreeing with Him and returning to a love relationship with Him. He prefers that you feel the grief that He feels. When you have a broken heart over your sin, you will want to do something about it: "Godly grief produces a repentance not to be regretted and leading to salvation" (2 Corinthians 7:10). Confession is agreeing with God about the real you and responding to God's holiness. Prayers of confession include seeking God's cleansing and forgiveness.

③ What emotion does God want you to feel about your sin? _____

④ In Proverbs 28:13 and 1 John 1:9 in the margin, underline God's promises if we confess our sins.

⑤ Read Hebrews 4:16 in the margin. How should we approach God to receive His mercy and grace? _____

The New Testament uses the word *forgiveness* in two ways. One is the legal sense of forgiveness. Jesus' death on the cross takes care of every sin a believer ever commits: past, present, and future. His sacrifice was all-sufficient. When you sin, you know it is already forgiven from a legal standpoint.

Sin in your life, however, stops the process of becoming like God. Sin breaks your fellowship and intimacy with God. First John 1:9 speaks of the relational sense of forgiveness. When you respond to God's holiness by agreeing with Him about your sin, He promises to give mercy, forgiveness, and cleansing. He restores the relationship of intimacy. Hebrews 4:16 encourages you to seek this mercy with boldness and confidence. Hebrews 10:19-22 describes the way you can enter God's presence:

> Since we have boldness to enter the sanctuary through the blood of Jesus, by the new and living way that He has inaugurated for us, through the curtain (that is, His flesh); and since we have a great high priest over the house of God, let us draw near with a true heart in full assurance of faith, our hearts sprinkled clean from an evil conscience and our bodies washed in pure water.

Because of Jesus you can enter God's presence with boldness and assurance. Develop the habit of agreeing with God so that when you sin, you are grieved and you immediately agree with Him about your sin and seek His forgiveness and restoration of fellowship.

 Pray, asking God to reveal sin in your life that hinders your relationship with Him. Use the sample prayer of confession in the right margin to agree with God about your sin. Be specific. Seek God's cleansing and restoration. Ask Him to make you holy, as He is holy. Also see biblical examples of confession on pages 92–93.

Proverbs 28:13
"The one who conceals his sins will not prosper, but whoever confesses and renounces them will find mercy."

1 John 1:9
"If we confess our sins, He is faithful and righteous to forgive us our sins and to cleanse us from all unrighteousness."

Hebrews 4:16
"Let us approach the throne of grace with boldness, so that we may receive mercy and find grace to help us at the proper time."

Sample Prayer of Confession
Lord, I don't feel what You feel, but I would like to. Help me feel the divine grief that You feel about my sin. Father, what I have done is not like You. And it is not like the real me that I am becoming in You. I want to agree with You about my sin and to become more like the real me, the eternal me that You want me to become. Cleanse me and restore me. Continue Your work in me. Make me holy, as You are holy. Amen.

Day 2 • Praise: Responding to God's Attributes

① According to yesterday's lesson, what is one kind of responding prayer that helps prepare you to enter God's presence? _____

One way to prepare to enter the throne room of heaven in prayer is confession. Through confession you receive cleansing and are restored to a right relationship with God. Confession is agreeing with God about the real you. You may object, "You don't know the real me. I don't want to be like the real me." Just one minute! The world tells you that you are a product of your past. If you agree with the world, that is the limit of the kind of person you will be—and that may not be very good. Christianity, however, teaches that you are a product of your future—what you are becoming. God is molding you into the image of His Son, Jesus Christ. As a Christian, you are becoming like Him. You are growing toward what you will be in eternity. Think of yourself in terms of eternity. This is the self about whom you want to agree with God in prayer.

↕ **Pause to pray. Fix in your mind an image of what Jesus is like—pure, loving, kind, holy, wise, patient, humble, and gentle. Spend time in confession. Agree with God that the person you are becoming is more like Jesus in these ways.**

A second kind of responding prayer is praise. In many different ways God reveals to you what He is like. His character traits are called His attributes. Praise is lifting up the attributes of God. You tend to become like what you value or praise. By lifting up God's attributes in praise, you respond to God by becoming more like Him.

② **Read in the margin the examples of praise. Pray them as you read. Circle or underline God's attributes.**

Do you see that praise focuses on who God is or what He is like? He is righteous, most high, strong and mighty, merciful, good, loving, wonderful, and faithful. These are just a few of God's attributes.

③ **Read the list of God's attributes in the right margin. Circle the ones that are particularly meaningful to you.**

Today's Prayer Promise

"If we confess our sins, He is faithful and righteous to forgive us our sins and to cleanse us from all unrighteousness."

Examples of Praise

"I will thank the LORD for His righteousness" (Psalm 7:17).

"Be exalted, LORD, in Your strength; we will sing and praise Your might" (Psalm 21:13).

"I trust in God's faithful love forever and ever. I will praise You forever for what You have done. In the presence of Your faithful people, I will put my hope in Your name, for it is good" (Psalm 52:8-9).

"My lips will glorify You because Your faithful love is better than life. So I will praise You as long as I live" (Psalm 63:3-4).

"LORD, the heavens praise Your wonders—Your faithfulness also" (Psalm 89:5).

④ **Fill in the blanks to describe a second kind of responding prayer.**
P _____ is responding to God's a_____.

⑤ Which is the purpose of responding prayers like praise?
○ a. I identify with God by working with Him in His kingdom.
○ b. I identify with God by becoming like Him.

When you pray, take time to offer praise to God. Respond to God's attributes by lifting them up. God wants you to become like Him. As you praise Him, ask Him to help you become more like Him. Allow God to remove every characteristic that is not like Him.

Praise is not just for the good times in your life. The writer of Hebrews said, "Through Him [Jesus] let us continually offer up to God a sacrifice of praise" (Hebrews 13:15). Praising God for who He is and for what He is like should be an attitude of your heart. You can praise Him continually.

Paul and Silas, for example, were beaten and thrown into jail for taking a stand for Jesus Christ. Would you praise God at a time like that? Read what they did: "About midnight Paul and Silas were praying and singing hymns to God, and the prisoners were listening to them" (Acts 16:25). Praise is insisting on the truth of God's nature regardless of the circumstances. God never changes. He is always worthy of our praise.

You will find that prayers of praise and worship are closely related. Praise focuses on His attributes. Worship focuses on the evidence of His attributes—His glory. Praise and worship prayers blend together as you pray.

 Using the attributes listed in this lesson and the biblical examples on pages 94–95, spend a few minutes praising God. You may want to use some of the biblical words for praise and worship below.

BIBLICAL WORDS FOR PRAISE AND WORSHIP

praise	hallelujah	alleluia	hosanna	magnify
exalt	rejoice	exult	ascribe	bless
laud	worship	adore	honor	glorify

Attributes of God

• able	• almighty
• attentive	• awesome
• beautiful	• blameless
• blessed	• enthroned
• eternal	• exalted
• faithful	• first
• flawless	• forgiving
• gentle	• glorious
• good	• gracious
• healing	• holy
• invisible	• jealous
• just	• kind
• last	• light
• living	• majestic
• merciful	• mighty
• patient	• peaceful
• perfect	• protective
• pure	• radiant
• righteous	• spirit
• strong	• supreme
• sure	• tender
• true	• unique
• wise	• wonderful

• abounding in love
• all-knowing
• all-powerful
• compassionate
• ever present
• has authority
• has integrity
• indescribable
• slow to anger
• understanding
• unfailing love
• worthy of praise

Praise is insisting
on the truth.

Day 3 • Worship: Responding to God's Glory

A third kind of responding prayer is worship. In the New Testament the Greek word for **worship*** derives from root words meaning *to kiss toward*. It is an act of obeisance, homage, reverence, or love.

Today's Prayer Promise
"Open your mouth wide, and I will fill it" (Psalm 81:10).

* *worship:* "to kiss toward," expressions of obeisance, homage, reverence, love, and adoration

① **List the first three kinds of responding prayers.**
   1. C _____
   2. P _____
   3. W _____
   4. Thanksgiving

God is not like any other. He reveals to us His beauty, brightness, and splendor—His glory—as He shows His attributes. God's actions reveal His glory. The Bible indicates that the heavens and the earth declare God's glory. Creation is the evidence of God's great creative power, His beauty, His wisdom, and much more.

When God reveals His glory, you recognize His worth—His surpassing value. You want to fall down and worship Him, love Him, and adore Him. You long to be with Him. You respond to God's glory through prayers of worship. You worship by expressing your reverence, honor, love, and adoration for God.

You respond to God's glory through prayers of worship.

Read on pages 96–97 some prayers of worship from the Bible. Pray them as you read them. Think of God's beauty and majesty as you pray.

② Write your own one-sentence prayer of worship.

_____

Expressing Prayers of Worship
1. Describe your reverence for God.
2. Magnify the Lord.
3. Exalt the Lord.
4. Ascribe to the Lord the glory due Him.
5. Bless the Lord.
6. Glorify the Lord.

Prayers of worship and praise go together. As you pray, you will find yourself focusing on God's attributes and praising Him. When you reflect on who God is and how He has revealed Himself, you will worship and adore Him. Worship begins with reverence for God.

Here are some ways you can express prayers of worship.
1. Describe your holy reverence for God. Acknowledge and honor His presence. Do not treat God's presence casually or lightly.

2. Magnify the Lord. Make Him bigger. The word *magnify* indicates perspective. You cannot make God bigger than He is. However, when you decrease yourself and magnify Him, He increases. That is what Mary did when she prayed: "My soul doth magnify the Lord. For he hath regarded the low estate of his handmaiden" (Luke 1:46,48, KJV). Focus on God's greatness in comparison to who you are.
3. Exalt the Lord. Make Him higher. John said of Jesus, "He must increase, but I must decrease" (John 3:30).
4. Ascribe to the Lord the glory due Him. Give God proper credit for what He has done. Do not accept His glory as your own.
5. Bless the Lord. Speak well of Him.
6. Glorify the Lord. Give Him honor and glory in what you say.

 Read in the margin the sample prayers of worship. Underline those that express your feelings of worship. Now pray them to the Lord.

Prayers of worship are responses to God's glory. Because God is spirit, you must worship God in spirit. The opposite of spirit is flesh, which can taint worship when you focus on self. Pride and arrogance before God prevent true worship. The real test in worship is this: Who is first? Who is foremost? To worship in spirit, think of God first. Seek to meet God, to see Him, to think about Him, to please Him, to fix your mind on Him. Flesh will lead you astray. Spirit will always lead you to God's supremacy. God's glory is very sacred. You dare not give His glory to another or take it for yourself, for God said:

> I am Yahweh, that is My name;
> I will not give My glory to another (Isaiah 42:8).

God's glory, demonstrated in your life, is the greatest good that can come to you. His glory is best demonstrated when your life reflects His character. The way you live your life can demonstrate worship to God by glorifying Him. God wants you to attain maturity, to reach the measure of the stature of Christ, and to become complete in Christ. When you worship the Lord, God works in you to make you more like Him.

 Close today's study by worshiping the Lord. Focus on Him as you express your reverence, awe, love, and adoration. Use the words at the end of day 2 if you wish.

Sample Prayers of Worship

- I bless You, Lord.
- Honor and majesty belong to You.
- I stand in awe of Your greatness and power.
- I love You because You first loved me.
- I long to be with You, Lord. I hunger and thirst for You.
- I would rather be a door-keeper in Your house than live as a rich person with the wicked.
- I glorify Your name because You have done great things.
- The heavens declare Your glory, Lord. I worship You in the splendor of Your holiness.
- The earth is full of Your glory, Lord. Your wisdom, knowledge, and power are beyond my understanding.
- Lord, Your splendor and majesty are glorious. I worship You.
- I long to be with You in eternity. I yearn for my redemption to be complete in Christ.
- I desire intimate fellowship with You.

Day 4 • Thanksgiving: Responding to God's Riches

Today's Prayer Promise

"Every generous act and every perfect gift is from above, coming down from the Father" (James 1:17).

Ephesians 1:3-9,11

"Blessed be the God and Father of our Lord Jesus Christ, who has blessed us with every spiritual blessing in the heavens, in Christ; He chose us in Him, before the foundation of the world, to be holy and blameless in His sight. In love He predestined us to be adopted through Jesus Christ for Himself, according to His favor and will, to the praise of His glorious grace that He favored us with in the Beloved. In Him we have redemption through His blood, the forgiveness of our trespasses, according to the riches of His grace that He lavished on us with all wisdom and understanding. He made known to us the mystery of His will, according to His good pleasure that He planned in Him In Him we were also made His inheritance, predestined according to the purpose of the One who works out everything in agreement with the decision of His will."

Squeezing toothpaste onto my toothbrush one morning, I (T. W.) realized that I had never thanked God for toothpaste. Come to think of it, I had never thanked Him for my teeth. I wondered, *What if my blessings tomorrow depended on my thanksgiving today? It would mean that if I did not thank God for air and lungs today, there would be no air tomorrow, and my lungs would collapse!*

Few of us realize our total dependence on God. We fail to acknowledge God as the source of everything we have. He is our source for abundant living, bestowing on us material and spiritual blessings according to His grace.

1. **Read today's prayer promise, James 1:17. Where does every generous act and perfect gift come from?** _____

2. **Read Ephesians 1:3-9,11 in the margin and underline some spiritual blessings God has given you. We've underlined one for you.**

Every good gift comes from God. He has blessed you with all spiritual blessings. God has chosen and adopted you as a child, has forgiven your sins, has given you wisdom and understanding, has revealed His will, and has given you an inheritance.

When God reveals Himself by giving blessings to you, thanksgiving to Him is a natural response. Thanksgiving is not just an act or a statement. It is an attitude of gratitude. Thanksgiving indicates a relationship between God as source and you as receiver. Prayers of thanksgiving indicate one of the most important characteristics of your relationship with God. Your relationship can grow only when you properly acknowledge that you are the receiver and God is the Giver.

3. **Read Ephesians 5:20 and Philippians 4:6 in the right margin. What does Paul say about gratitude?**
   ○ a. Thank God for only the good things in life.
   ○ b. Thank God for every situation—both good and difficult.
   ○ c. Thanksgiving is not important unless you want something.

Paul tells us always to be thankful in every situation (b). This is difficult for most of us. We think of gratitude merely as a reaction to a favor, not to unpleasant events. Properly expressing gratitude means that you thank God in all circumstances—large and small, good and bad. Response to God in gratitude should be a continuous attitude of your heart: "Give thanks in everything, for this is God's will for you in Christ Jesus" (1 Thessalonians 5:18).

Learning to be content in whatever state in which you find yourself helps you submit to God's sovereignty. He wants you to develop gratitude for all you have rather than to focus on what you do not have. Thanksgiving is responding to God for the blessings He has bestowed on you.

Gratitude is a continuous attitude about your relationship with the One who continuously gives to you, supplies your needs, and brings you joy. Gratitude is a response not only to what God does but also to who God is. Gratitude is the heart's response to God's goodness—not merely to the gifts of His goodness but also to His quality of goodness.

④ **What quality of God encourages our gratitude?** _____

⑤ **Turn to pages 98–99 and read the examples of thanksgiving. In the space provided on those pages, list from Scripture some things for which you can thank God.**

God's nature is good. His will and work are always good. You can thank God for even the difficult or trying experiences in life, knowing that He can work through those for your good (see Romans 8:28 in the margin). Here are some other things for which you can thank God: spiritual riches, honor, strength, His nearness, His wonderful works, joy and gladness, freedom, daily provision, a call to be involved in His work, and wisdom.

⑥ **Read in the margin the list of subjects for thanks. List on page 99 other things, persons, or experiences for which you can give thanks.**

↕ **Pray through your lists and use the Scriptures on pages 98–99 to express your gratitude to God for His goodness and for all He is and does for you. Be alert to ways to express your gratitude to God today.**

Ephesians 5:20
"… giving thanks always for everything to God the Father in the name of our Lord Jesus Christ."

Philippians 4:6
"In everything, through prayer and petition with thanksgiving, let your requests be made known to God."

Gratitude is a response not only to what God does but also to who God is.

Romans 8:28
"All things work together for the good of those who love God: those who are called according to His purpose."

Subjects for Thanks
- Redemption, mercy, grace, forgiveness
- Meaningful spiritual experiences
- Family, relatives, friends, and church
- Provision for your needs
- Persons and events that have had spiritual impacts on your life

Day 5 • Responding Together

Today's Prayer Promise

"Come, let us discuss this," says the LORD. "Though your sins are like scarlet, they will be as white as snow; though they are as red as crimson, they will be like wool" (Isaiah 1:18).

Nehemiah 9:1-3

"The Israelites assembled; they were fasting, wearing sackcloth, and had put dust on their heads. Those of Israelite descent separated themselves from all foreigners, and they stood and confessed their sins and the guilt of their fathers. While they stood in their places, they read from the book of the law of the LORD their God for a fourth of the day and spent another fourth of the day in confession and worship of the LORD their God."

James 5:16

"Confess your sins to one another and pray for one another, so that you may be healed. The intense prayer of the righteous is very powerful."

You will spend most of this week's prayer session in responding prayers. Today you will prepare for your small-group prayer session.

PREPARING TO CONFESS

In Isaiah 1:18, today's prayer promise, God invites you to reason together with Him about your sin. No matter how bad the sin appears, He can cleanse and forgive! Confession is a way to respond to God's holiness by agreeing with Him and turning away from your sin. As you do, God makes you holy—set apart for His work.

Sometimes sin needs to be confessed publicly (see Nehemiah 9:1-3 in the margin). This is especially true when a group has sinned. We call this corporate sin.

1. **Circle sins that could be church sins or group sins rather than individual sins. Some could be both.**

pride	murder	robbery	sexual immorality
envy	adultery	bribery	tolerating evil
greed	unbelief	unforgiveness	shifting priority from God
lying	gossip	bitterness	neglecting the needy

Nearly all of these could be sins of a church or a group. Some, however, like murder, robbery, sexual immorality, adultery, bribery, lying, and gossip, are more likely to be individual sins. James 5:16, in the margin, commands us to confess our sins to one another. Healing and deliverance can come when others pray for you about an area of sin, weakness, need, or fault. Take care, however, when you confess sin publicly. Below are some guidelines to follow when confessing sin to others.

Guidelines for Confession

1. Confession should be directed by the Holy Spirit.
2. Limit group confession to what is corporately (as a group) agreed on as sin.
3. Corporate confession is not accusation of others but agreement with God and with one another that the action confessed is sin.
4. Confession includes sins of omission and commission.

5. The purpose of confessing personal sin is to secure forgiveness or to enlist prayer support.

6. Any sin that has caused damage to a group should be publicly confessed.

7. The circle of confession should be as wide as the circle of damage done by the sin.

8. Confession should not be public when it would hurt other persons or lead to anger or lust.

(2) **Confession also includes agreeing with God about truth. Turn to page 93 and read two examples of the confession of truth. Now read in the margin the list of sample prayers of the confession of truth. In the margin or on page 93, list other truths you can confess about God or about who you are in relation to God.**

PREPARING TO PRAISE

During your group prayer time this week, you will respond to God's attributes in praise. You might use statements like these: "I praise You, Lord, for You are. … " "I magnify Your name because You are. …"

(3) **List four or more attributes of God for which you can praise Him. If you need to, skim Psalms to find some of His attributes.**

_____

_____

_____

_____

PREPARING TO WORSHIP

(4) **Turn to pages 96–97 and select an example of worship that is meaningful to you. Underline what the Scripture describes of God's glory.**

PREPARING TO GIVE THANKS

(5) **Review the lists on pages 41 and 99 of things for which you can express thanks to God. Draw a star beside those for which you are particularly thankful.**

↕ **Spend a few minutes in prayer, responding to God's holiness, attributes, glory, and riches.**

Sample Prayers of the Confession of Truth

- Sin no longer has dominion over me.
- You have dressed me in robes of Your righteousness.
- You are Lord and Master; I am Your servant.
- You are my Father; I am Your child.
- You are Sovereign; my answer is yes.
- You are Truth; You are my Way and Life.
- I walk in victory with Christ.
- Greater is He who is in me than he who is in the world.

Week 4

Asking Prayers

"Don't worry about anything, but in everything, through prayer and petition with thanksgiving, let your requests be made known to God"

Philippians 4:6

Asking Prayers

OVERVIEW OF WEEK 4
Day 1: Praying for Yourself and Others
Day 2: Reasons God Answers Prayer
Day 3: Reasons God Doesn't Answer Prayer
Day 4: Principles for Asking
Day 5: Agreeing Together

VERSE TO MEMORIZE
"Don't worry about anything, but in everything, through prayer and petition with thanksgiving, let your requests be made known to God" (Philippians 4:6).

DISCIPLESHIP HELPS FOR WEEK 4
"Suggestions for Praying Together" (p. 110)

PREVIEW OF WEEK 4
This week begins a focus on asking prayers: petition and intercession. Jesus taught much about asking prayers. This week you will—
• understand the importance of asking and of agonizing in prayer;
• consider biblical examples to identify reasons God does and does not answer prayer;
• apply biblical truths to improve the effectiveness of your prayer life;
• understand basic principles for asking prayers;
• learn how to pray in agreement with others as you pray together.

Day 1 • Praying for Yourself and Others

Scripture-Memory Verse

"Don't worry about anything, but in everything, through prayer and petition with thanksgiving, let your requests be made known to God" (Philippians 4:6).

You have now completed half of your study of *Pray in Faith*. Let's review what you have learned.

1. **Can you recite your three memory verses? Check the boxes beside the verses you can recite successfully.**
   ○ Matthew 21:22   ○ Matthew 18:19   ○ Hebrews 13:15

2. **Name four kinds of responding prayers and the aspects of God's nature to which you respond. Check your answers on page 91.**
   _____ is responding to God's _____.
   _____ is responding to God's _____.
   _____ is responding to God's _____.
   _____ is responding to God's _____.

3. **What is the purpose of responding prayers?**
   ○ a. I identify with God by working with Him in His kingdom.
   ○ b. I identify with God by becoming like Him.

4. **What are two kinds of asking prayers?**
   _____ is asking for myself that is led by my Father.
   _____ is asking for others that is led by my Master.

5. **Which of the following is the purpose of asking prayers?**
   ○ a. I identify with God by working with Him in His kingdom.
   ○ b. I identify with God by becoming like Him.

We have studied four types of responding prayers. In confession, praise, worship, and thanksgiving you identify with God by becoming like Him. Now we will focus on asking prayers: petition and intercession. In asking prayers you identify with God by working with Him in His kingdom.

GOD'S WAY OF WORKING

Many years ago when I (T. W.) served in the Korean War, very few Koreans were Christians—less than 1 percent. But they prayed fervently and faithfully. Prayer was their very life. Today more than 33 percent of Koreans are Christians. Do you know why? Because they are praying, and God is

Answers: 3–b, 5–a

answering. In fact, they may be the most prayerful people in the world. God is honoring their prayers.

All around the world God is moving. He is moving mightily where people are praying. Do you know what the problem is where people are not responding to the gospel? The body of Christ is in poor spiritual condition. We are not praying. We are not seeing the great work of God. God's work must be done on God's basis. That is the only way He will work. Jesus repeatedly emphasized the method for accomplishing God's work: we must ask.

⑥ Read the Scriptures in the margin. Circle the word *ask* in each verse.

Real prayer is difficult. It is work. We are so comfortable, however, that we don't want to fight. We are failing in Kingdom work because we are not fighting. Paul begged the Roman Christians to "agonize together with me in your prayers to God on my behalf" (Romans 15:30). In writing to the Colossian church, Paul said, "Epaphras … is always contending for you in his prayers, so that you can stand mature and fully assured in everything God wills" (Colossians 4:12). I don't know very many who strive or wrestle in prayer. Not only do we need individual prayer warriors today, but we also need churches that are houses of prayer.

⑦ Check the better description of the kind of prayer needed today.
    ○ a. We need prayer that is easy. If little time or effort is required, many more people will agree to pray.
    ○ b. We need agonizing, fervent prayer. Much time and great effort are required for the kind of results needed today.

The church needs agonizing, fervent prayer. Perhaps sin has become so common among God's people that God does not hear our prayers. Instead of getting right with God, we have stopped praying. We are not even asking. We are not achieving victories for Christ. We are not doing God's work on God's basis.

 Ask God to begin showing you the kind of prayer He wants of you. Ask Him to stir your heart to agonizing, fervent prayer for His kingdom's sake. Pray for your church to become a house of prayer.

God Invites Asking

"Keep asking, and it will be given to you. Keep searching, and you will find. Keep knocking, and the door will be opened to you" (Matthew 7:7).

"If you ask Me anything in My name, I will do it" (John 14:14).

"If you remain in Me and My words remain in you, ask whatever you want and it will be done for you" (John 15:7).

"Until now you have asked for nothing in My name. Ask and you will receive, that your joy may be complete" (John 16:24).

Day 2 • Reasons God Answers Prayer

Today's Prayer Promise

"In that day you will not ask Me anything. I assure you: Anything you ask the Father in My name, He will give you. Until now you have asked for nothing in My name. Ask and you will receive, that your joy may be complete" (John 16:23-24).

God's Honor

"If You kill this people with a single blow, the nations that have heard of Your fame will declare, 'Since the LORD wasn't able to bring this people into the land He swore to give them, He has slaughtered them in the wilderness'" (Numbers 14:15-16).

God's Glory

"My soul is troubled. What should I say—Father, save Me from this hour? But that is why I came to this hour. Father, glorify Your name!" (John 12:27-28).

The great prayer warriors of the Bible often told God why He should answer their prayers. Seeking God's viewpoint, they desired to pray for what God wanted to do. Today you will learn some reasons God answers prayer.

1. Read the following eight reasons God answers prayer. Underline a word or two in each one to help you remember it.

1. The prayer seeks to uphold God's honor. God's honor means His good name, reputation, or integrity. In some prayers you may seek to maintain the integrity of God's character and His name. After the faithless report of the spies who were sent into the promised land, God threatened to slay the Israelites. Moses prayed on behalf of God's honor, expressing a desire to protect God's reputation among the surrounding nations (see Numbers 14:15-16 in the margin).

2. The prayer appeals for God's glory. God's glory invites worshipful praise. His glory is His magnificence, His great beauty or splendor, or the evidence of His attributes. In some prayers you may ask that God reveal or receive His glory. We dare not give His glory to another or take it for ourselves. The men and women of the Bible were always diligent to ensure that divine work was recognized as truly from God—they gave God the glory. Jesus prayed for His Father's glory (see John 12:27-28) instead of seeking His own desires.

3. The prayer appeals to God's character. God's character refers to His traits, qualities, or nature. You can agree with God about His nature in prayer. You can also ask Him to act according to His nature. Moses made a request based on God's character, identifying several of His qualities (see Numbers 14:17-19). Because God is merciful, forgiving, and long-suffering, Moses asked God to pardon and forgive the people.

4. The prayer acknowledges God's sovereignty. God's sovereignty means His supreme power, rank, or authority over all. He is Ruler over all. As Sennacherib gathered his Assyrian army against Judah, King Hezekiah acknowledged God's sovereignty over all kingdoms of the earth. He realized that a positive answer to his request would cause all of the kingdoms to recognize that truth as well (see 2 Kings 19:15,19).

5. Jesus prays for you. Have you ever asked a godly person to pray for you, thinking that God would surely hear? You have an even better reason for God to answer your request: Jesus Himself prays for you! Paul tells us, "Christ Jesus … is at the right hand of God and intercedes for us" (Romans 8:34). Because Jesus is interested in you, He supports you in every appropriate prayer you utter and seeks God's very best for you.

6. *The Holy Spirit prays with and for you according to God's will.* Your greatest weakness in prayer may be that you do not know what or how to ask. But here's good news: "The Spirit also joins to help in our weakness, because we do not know what to pray for as we should, but the Spirit Himself intercedes for us … according to the will of God" (Romans 8:26-27). The Holy Spirit knows God's will and guides you to pray according to God's will.

7. *Your Father wants to answer the requests of His child.* God answers prayer because of who you are in relation to Him. Jesus commanded you to pray to God as Father: "Our Father in heaven" (Matthew 6:9). Your relationship as a child of God ought to influence the way you pray. God hears you because you are His child.

8. *Your Master wants to answer the requests of His servant.* You can also pray on the basis of being God's servant. The cause of God cannot be separated from that of His servants. If you are His servant, your prayers touch His work and interest Him. After the dedication of the temple, Solomon prayed as a servant to his Master (see 1 Kings 8:59-60).

Pray and ask God to teach you how to pray from His viewpoint. List one of your most important prayer requests today. Review the eight reasons God answers prayer and state why God would want to answer your prayer. Ask God what He wants you to pray for. Then pray from God's viewpoint, stating His reasons for answering your request.

Prayer request: _____

_____

_____

Reasons for God to answer: _____

_____

_____

_____

God's Character

"Just as You have spoken: The LORD is slow to anger and rich in faithful love, forgiving wrongdoing and rebellion. … Please pardon the wrongdoing of this people in keeping with the greatness of Your faithful love, just as You have forgiven them from Egypt until now" (Numbers 14:17-19).

God's Sovereignty

"LORD God of Israel who is enthroned above the cherubim, You are God—You alone—of all the kingdoms of the earth. You made the heavens and the earth. Now, LORD our God, please save us from his hand so that all the kingdoms of the earth may know that You are the LORD God—You alone" (2 Kings 19:15,19).

Master-Servant

"May my words … be near the LORD our God day and night, so that He may uphold His servant's cause and … so that all the peoples of the earth may know that the LORD is God. There is no other!" (1 Kings 8:59-60).

Day 3 • Reasons God Doesn't Answer Prayer

Today's Prayer Promise

"If our hearts do not condemn us we have confidence before God, and can receive whatever we ask from Him because we keep His commands and do what is pleasing in His sight" (1 John 3:21-22).

Psalm 66:18

"If I had cherished sin in my heart, the Lord would not have listened" (NIV).

Isaiah 59:1-2

"The LORD's hand is not too short to save, and His ear is not too deaf to hear. But your iniquities have built barriers between you and your God, and your sins have made Him hide His face from you so that He does not listen."

Hebrews 3:12,18-19

"Watch out, brothers, so that there won't be in any of you an evil, unbelieving heart that departs from the living God. And to whom did He 'swear that they would not enter His rest,' if not those who disobeyed? So we see that they were unable to enter because of unbelief."

Any sin is serious and hinders prayer. We want to avoid all sin, but we are wise to give special attention to sins the Bible specifically identifies as hindrances to prayer.

1. Read the Scriptures in the left and right margins (Psalm 66:18; Isaiah 59:1-2; Hebrews 3:12,18-19; James 1:5-8; 4:2-3). Underline reasons God doesn't answer prayer or actions that hinder prayer.

2. Below is a list of sins that are reasons God doesn't answer prayer or says no, followed by a series of Scriptures. Match the sin with the Scripture that mentions it by writing one or more references beside each sin.

Anger/wrath: _____

Broken relationships: _____

Doubting/unbelief: _____

Hypocrisy: _____

Idolatry: _____

Indifference to need: _____

Unforgiveness: _____

Ezekiel 14:3 • "Son of man, these men have set up idols in their hearts and have put sinful stumbling blocks before their faces. Should I be consulted by them at all?"

Proverbs 21:13 • "The one who shuts his ears to the cry of the poor will himself also call out and not be answered."

Matthew 5:23-24 • "If you are offering your gift on the altar, and there you remember that your brother has something against you, leave your gift there in front of the altar. First go and be reconciled with your brother, and then come and offer your gift."

Matthew 6:5 • "Whenever you pray, you must not be like the hypocrites, because they love to pray standing in the synagogues and on the street corners to be seen by people. I assure you: They've got their reward!"

Matthew 6:14-15 • "If you forgive people their wrongdoing, your heavenly Father will forgive you as well. But if you don't forgive people, your Father will not forgive your wrongdoing."

1 Timothy 2:8 • "I will therefore that men pray every where, lifting up holy hands, without wrath and doubting" (KJV).

1 Peter 3:7 • "Husbands, in the same way, live with your wives with understanding of their weaker nature yet showing them honor as co-heirs of the grace of life, so that your prayers will not be hindered."

 Examine the following list of sins and hindrances to prayer. Ask God to show you any area of your life that may be a barrier in your prayer life. If He shows you anything, confess it. Seek His forgiveness and determine to walk in a new way. Check off each area as you allow God to examine it. Take as much time for this process as God may require.

○ Anger/wrath   ○ Broken relationships

○ Doubting/unbelief   ○ Hypocrisy

○ Idolatry (idols of the heart)   ○ Indifference to need

○ Iniquities (moral crookedness)   ○ Sins

○ Unforgiveness   ○ Wrong or selfish motives

James 1:5-8

"If any of you lacks wisdom, he should ask God, who gives to all generously and without criticizing, and it will be given to him. But let him ask in faith without doubting. For the doubter is like the surging sea, driven and tossed by the wind. That person should not expect to receive anything from the Lord. An indecisive man is unstable in all his ways."

James 4:2-3

"You desire and do not have. You murder and covet and cannot obtain. You fight and war. You do not have because you do not ask. You ask and don't receive because you ask wrongly, so that you may spend it on your desires for pleasure."

#2 answers:
anger/wrath: 1 Timothy 2:8;
broken relationships:
Matthew 5:23-24; 1 Peter 3:7;
doubting/unbelief: 1 Timothy 2:8;
hypocrisy: Matthew 6:5;
idolatry: Ezekiel 14:3;
indifference to need: Proverbs 21:13;
unforgiveness: Matthew 6:14-15

Day 4 • Principles for Asking

In the Bible God gives us some guidelines for asking prayers. Today we will study 10 principles for asking.

① **As you read the principles below, read the corresponding Scriptures in the margins.**

1. *Ask in the Spirit.* This means that every request proceeds from the mind of the Spirit, not from selfish motives or self-serving ends. Praying in the Spirit is directly related to praying according to His will.

2. *Ask according to His will.* Our weakness in prayer is this: "We do not know what to pray for as we should, but the Spirit Himself intercedes for us … according to the will of God" (Romans 8:26-27). Ask according to God's will with the help of the Holy Spirit. When you don't know what to ask, keep praying and seeking God's direction for your request.

3. *Ask with the mind.* Your mind helps you form your requests and make them precise and specific. This is one reason to list prayer requests in a notebook. A prayer list keeps your mind from wandering as you pray and enables you to pray specifically and persistently until the answer comes.

② **List the first three principles of asking.**

1. Ask in _____

2. Ask according to _____

3. Ask with _____

4. *Ask in Jesus' name.* When you use Jesus' name, you claim to represent Him and act like Him—to have His desires, qualities, gratitude, and outlook. When you prepare to make a request, first ask yourself, *What would Jesus want in this situation?* Let His desires become your desires. Praying in Jesus' name also relates to praying according to His will.

5. *Ask while abiding in Christ.* Prayer is both a means and a result of abiding in Christ. To abide in Him, you continue in constant fellowship with Him, you pray without ceasing, and you obediently accept His will and Word for you. As a branch abides in the vine, a Christian abides in Christ. Spend time with Him in prayer and in His Word.

6. *Ask in faith.* Asking in faith means asking without doubt in your heart. Believe that the things you ask will come to pass. Reflect God's char-

Today's Prayer Promise

"Whatever you ask in My name, I will do it so that the Father may be glorified in the Son. If you ask Me anything in My name, I will do it" (John 14:13-14).

In the Spirit

"I will pray with the spirit" (1 Corinthians 14:15).

"Pray at all times in the Spirit" (Ephesians 6:18).

According to His Will

"This is the confidence we have before Him: whenever we ask anything according to His will, He hears us. And if we know that He hears whatever we ask, we know that we have what we have asked Him for" (1 John 5:14-15).

With the Mind

"I will also pray with my mind" (1 Corinthians 14:15, NIV).

In Jesus' Name

"If you ask Me anything in My name, I will do it" (John 14:14).

acter in always being the same. Recognize God's authority and power to answer in the way He chooses. Have confidence in God's care and purposes for your life. Finally, you can claim a God-given Bible promise and anticipate God's response.

③ **List three more principles of asking.**
   4. Ask in _____
   5. Ask while _____
   6. Ask in _____

7. ***Ask in humility.*** Praying in humility recognizes your need of God. Humility submits to God, whereas pride, arrogance, and independence prevent an attitude of humility. The secret to humility is to understand who God is. Pride always indicates that you have failed to perceive His greatness. Come to God recognizing His greatness and your need.

8. ***Ask in sincerity.*** When you pray in sincerity, your faith leads you to pray genuine, heartfelt prayers. You are so serious about your praying that your prayer is earnest and fervent, not fake or artificial.

9. ***Ask with perseverance.*** *Perseverance* means *persistence, not giving up.* God expects you to persevere in prayer to make you sure of what He wants and of what you want. He wants to train you to take your eyes off discouraging circumstances and to focus on Him. He also wants you to prove and establish earnestness and to demonstrate real faith.

10. ***Ask using God's words.*** Quote God's Word to Him. In this way you present God's own thoughts back to Him.

④ **List the last four principles of asking.**
   7. Ask in _____
   8. Ask in _____
   9. Ask with _____
   10. Ask using _____

 Review the 10 principles for asking. You may want to write them on an index card for regular review. Now spend some time with your Father and Master in prayer. As you phrase your requests, practice the principles for asking. Begin keeping a list of your requests so that you can pray with your mind. You can continue to expand your lists on pages 104–9.

Abiding in Christ
"If you remain in Me and My words remain in you, ask whatever you want and it will be done for you" (John 15:7).

In Faith
"Have faith in God. Therefore, I tell you, all the things you pray and ask for—believe that you have received them, and you will have them" (Mark 11:22,24).

In Humility
"[If] My people who are called by My name humble themselves, pray …" (2 Chronicles 7:14).

In Sincerity
"The intense prayer of the righteous is very powerful" (James 5:16).

With Perseverance
"Pray at all times in the Spirit, and stay alert in this, with all perseverance and intercession for all the saints" (Ephesians 6:18).

Day 5 • Agreeing Together

Today's Prayer Promise

"I assure you: Whatever you bind on earth is already bound in heaven, and whatever you loose on earth is already loosed in heaven. Again, I assure you: If two of you on earth agree about any matter that you pray for, it will be done for you by My Father in heaven" (Matthew 18:18-19).

James 1:6-7

"Let him ask in faith without doubting. For the doubter ... should not expect to receive anything from the Lord."

James 4:2-3

"You do not have because you do not ask. You ask and don't receive because you ask wrongly, so that you may spend it on your desires for pleasure."

Psalm 66:18

"If I had cherished sin in my heart, the Lord would not have listened" (NIV).

When your church or group prays together, God is present, and His people are present. United prayer includes a visible union (people gathered together) and an agreement of mind and heart. Agreeing together in prayer, however, is not just human agreement. God is involved. The kind of agreement we seek is agreeing with God in our requests. That kind of praying comes about only through the leadership of the Holy Spirit. When you agree with God in prayer, your request will be answered.

1) **Read in the margin today's prayer promise, Matthew 18:18-19. Underline the promise God makes to you when you pray with others in agreement.**

Jesus promised that if we pray in agreement, our Father will do what we ask. In addition, Jesus taught us to pray, "Your will be done on earth as it is in heaven" (Matthew 6:10). When we pray in agreement, we seek His will to be done on earth. In a sense we pray in this sequence:
1. "Our Father in heaven, what is Your will in this matter?"
2. The Holy Spirit guides us to know the mind of the Father.
3. We pray: "Father, we ask You to do that on earth according to Your wishes. We agree with Your purposes and ways."
4. God answers this prayer of agreement.

You may want to ask, How can we get to the point at which we can hear and respond in prayer that way? We believe the following process is part of agreeing with God in prayer.

GET INTO AGREEMENT WITH GOD
As we have already studied this week, sin, unbelief, and wrong motives hinder our relationship with God.

2) **Read James 1:6-7, James 4:2-3, and Psalm 66:18 in the margin and match the verses with the barriers that hinder answered prayer. Write a reference beside each barrier below.**
Sin: _____
Doubt/unbelief: _____
Wrong motives: _____

You cannot be in agreement with God when sin (Psalm 66:18), unbelief (James 1:6-7), and wrong motives (James 4:2-3) are prominent in your life. God chooses not to listen to and answer the prayers of such people. Consequently, such people are out of agreement with God (see diagram 1). The first step toward praying in agreement is to remove these barriers to your prayers. You need to get to the place where God is listening when you pray and you hear clearly when He speaks and leads. Make right your relationship with God, and you will be in a place of agreement with Him (see diagram 2).

All who are praying together must do the same. If one of you is wrong with the Lord, that broken relationship can hinder the whole group's prayer. Everyone in your group should be right with the Lord if you want to pray in agreement with Him.

 Pause to pray. Ask God to reveal any sin, unbelief, or wrong motives in your life that would hinder your relationship with Him. Pray by name for each member in your prayer group right now, asking God to help each person move to a right relationship with Him as well. Don't proceed until you have prayed.

GET INTO AGREEMENT WITH OTHERS

The early church spent much time praying together with one mind and one heart: "These were continually united in prayer" (Acts 1:14). "Every day they devoted themselves to meeting together in the temple complex, and broke bread from house to house. They ate their food with gladness and simplicity of heart, praising God" (Acts 2:46-47). "The multitude of those who believed were of one heart and soul, and no one said that any of his possessions was his own, but instead they held everything in common" (Acts 4:32). The church is a body, with every part dependent on the other parts. We need one another to function properly.

Pride, sin, and broken relationships can hinder our agreement with other believers (see diagram 3 on p. 56). Jesus said, "If you are offering your gift on the altar, and there you remember that your brother has something against you, leave your gift there in front of the altar. First go and be reconciled with your brother, and then come and offer your gift" (Matthew 5:23-24). Apply this same principle when you come to prayer. Until you are right with another person, you are not acceptable to the Lord. You cannot pray in agreement with another if anything is not right between you.

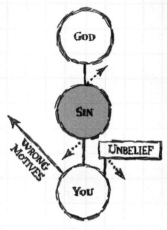

1. Out of Agreement with God

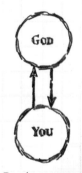

2. In Agreement with God

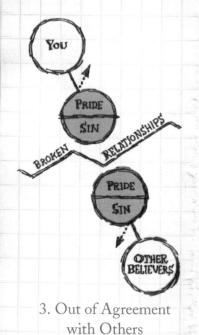

3. Out of Agreement
with Others

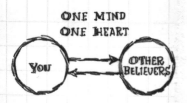

4. In Agreement
with Others

Many sins we studied in day 3 relate to others: anger, wrath, broken relationships, hypocrisy, indifference to need, iniquities (moral crookedness or failure), and unforgiveness.

Pride is also a major sin that may keep you from agreeing with others or from being reconciled with them. Pride may cause you to think you don't need your brothers and sisters in Christ. It may cause you to think you are closer to the Lord than they are; therefore, you don't pay much attention to what and how they pray. You must humble yourself and submit to one another to be of one heart and mind. You need to reconcile broken relationships and bring your life into unity and harmony with them (see diagram 4).

 Pray and ask God to reveal to you any sin or broken relationship that you may have with other believers. If He reveals anything, begin the process of seeking reconciliation. Write notes below about the things God brings to mind that need to be corrected.

_____

_____

SEEK GOD'S PERSPECTIVE AND PRAY IN AGREEMENT WITH GOD

After you and all of the believers praying with you are right with God and with one another, you are ready to pray in agreement. Look at diagrams 5 and 6 on page 57. Notice that you first seek God's perspective (5). You want to know what He desires in the matter about which you are praying. As you pray and seek the Lord's will in the matter, He will begin to reveal what is on His heart. Then pray in agreement with God. Let His desire become your request (6). God reveals what He wants to do. When you ask in agreement with Him, His answer is yes!

③ Review "Suggestions for Praying Together" on page 110. Underline key ideas that will help you and your group pray in agreement.

SUGGESTIONS FOR PRAYING TOGETHER THIS WEEK

Be specific in what you ask of God. Ask the Holy Spirit to guide your praying according to God's will. Pay attention to the direction in which the Holy Spirit prompts you to pray. As you begin to form your request on a subject, check your spirit for confirmation of what others are praying.

If a spirit of agreement prevails, express it. If a question or a doubt exists, express it. Don't hide questions or doubts from the Lord or from those with whom you are praying. These may lead to further praying, which may lead to the correct request.

Consider God's viewpoint and give God reasons to answer. Consider these possible reasons: the prayer request can—
1. uphold God's honor;
2. appeal for God's glory;
3. appeal to God's character;
4. acknowledge God's sovereignty.

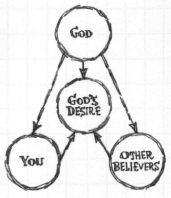

5. Agreeing with God

Ask yourselves, *What would Jesus ask for?* Remember that Jesus is praying with you and for you. Ask, "Holy Spirit, what do You want us to pray according to the Father's will?" Is this a request of a child to a Father or of a servant to a Master?

Use biblical principles, patterns, and promises to guide your requests. Pay attention to Scriptures that come to mind as you pray. They could be the Holy Spirit's promptings. When a person's prayer causes a Scripture to come to mind, pay attention to what God may be saying through that Scripture. If your spirit agrees with what someone is praying, then tell the Lord that you agree. These kinds of prayers will greatly increase your faith as you pray. God can and will guide you to pray in a specific direction so that you know the answer has been granted. Then you can wait in great expectation for the answer.

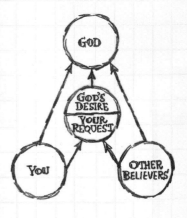

6. Praying in Agreement

Seek Spirit-guided agreement with others in your prayers. Don't settle for mere human agreement. Pray on major issues until you come to one heart and mind on a matter. Listen to the prayers of others for direction or answers to your prayers. Often, guidance or direction comes while you are praying, not before. If heartfelt agreement does not come, keep on praying for days and weeks until God gives direction.

 Conclude your study today by praying. Ask God to teach you and your prayer group how to pray in agreement. Ask Him to begin teaching you through your experience praying together this week.

Week 5

Petition

"Keep asking, and it will be given
to you. Keep searching, and you will
find. Keep knocking, and the
door will be opened to you"

Matthew 7:7

Petition

OVERVIEW OF WEEK 5
Day 1: Asking for Yourself
Day 2: A Model for Petition
Day 3: Following Your Father's Leading
Day 4: Praying for Yourself
Day 5: Asking Others to Pray for You

VERSE TO MEMORIZE
"Keep asking, and it will be given to you. Keep searching, and you will find.
Keep knocking, and the door will be opened to you" (Matthew 7:7).

DISCIPLESHIP HELPS FOR WEEK 5
"Prayers of Petition" (pp. 100–101)

PREVIEW OF WEEK 5
Petition is asking for yourself, your family, your group, or your church. Your Heavenly
Father leads your personal petition to mold you into the person He wants you to be.
This week you will—
• learn that God invites personal petition;
• use biblical examples to identify the kinds of petition that God invites, hears,
 and answers;
• understand God's purpose in helping you become the kind of person He desires;
• realize the importance of asking others to pray for you;
• learn ways to be specific in praying for others.

Day 1 • Asking for Yourself

Today's Prayer Promise

"We do not have a high priest who is unable to sympathize with our weaknesses, but One who has been tested in every way as we are, yet without sin. Therefore let us approach the throne of grace with boldness, so that we may receive mercy and find grace to help us at the proper time" (Hebrews 4:15-16).

Abram

"Abram said, 'Lord God, what can You give me, since I am childless and the heir of my house is Eliezer of Damascus?'" (Genesis 15:2).

Hannah

"Deeply hurt, Hannah prayed to the LORD and wept with many tears. Making a vow, she pleaded, 'LORD of Hosts, if You will take notice of Your servant's affliction, remember and not forget me, and give Your servant a son, I will give him to the LORD all the days of his life'" (1 Samuel 1:10-11).

During these final two weeks you will study the asking prayers in more detail. This week's lessons will focus on petition; next week's, on intercession. Before we begin a detailed look at petition, review last week's lessons.

1. On page 47 read again the Scriptures in the margin under "God Invites Asking."

2. On pages 48–49 read the eight reasons God answers prayer. Which two are most encouraging, meaningful, or helpful in your own praying? Write them below.

   _____

   _____

3. Name four reasons God doesn't answer prayer. Review pages 50–51 if you need help.

   _____

   _____

   _____

   _____

4. On pages 52–53 read the 10 principles for asking. In which principle do you most need improvement for the sake of your prayer life?

   _____

5. Of the following areas, on which one do you most need to work to improve your praying in agreement with God? Check one.
   ○ a. Getting into agreement with God
   ○ b. Getting into agreement with others
   ○ c. Understanding God's desires for a particular request
   ○ d. Praying with others long enough to agree together

Petition is asking for yourself, your family, your church, or your group. You might think that the great prayer warriors of the Bible did not emphasize personal petition. Yet many of them made personal petitions. In Genesis 15:2 Abram (later Abraham) asked God for a son. In 1 Samuel 1:10-11 Hannah prayed for a son. King Hezekiah was dying and prayed to live (see 2 Kings 20:1-3). Zechariah and Elizabeth prayed for a child (see Luke 1:13). God heard and answered all of these personal petitions.

⑥ **Based on these biblical examples, which of the following is true?**
○ a. Personal petition is selfish. God doesn't want us to pray for personal concerns.
○ b. Personal petition is acceptable to the Lord since He answers and even encourages these personal requests.

The examples in the Bible indicate that God is pleased to hear your personal requests. God's purpose in encouraging petition is to mold you into a certain kind of person. In each example in the margin, the person praying was in the process of becoming a more godly person. Abraham didn't just receive a son; God gave him a nation. Hannah was becoming a certain kind of person when she prayed for a son, for motherhood changes the character of a woman of God. Hezekiah became one of Israel's greatest kings.

⑦ **What is a primary purpose in God's encouraging personal petition?**

_____

_____

In each case of personal petition above, not only the person but also God's work and kingdom benefited. Abraham's prayer resulted in the chosen race that would prepare the way for Christ. Hannah's prayer gave to Israel Samuel, a great judge and the first prophet. Because he did not die as soon as predicted, Hezekiah lived to father Manasseh. In so doing, he preserved the messianic line of David that led to the birth of Jesus. God shapes your character and uses you to join His kingdom work.

⬍ **Close today's study by thanking your Father for specific ways He has helped you become the person He wants you to be. Ask Him to continue showing you direction for your life. Begin to fix your thoughts on Jesus—your perfect example of godly living.**

Hezekiah

"In those days Hezekiah became terminally ill. The prophet Isaiah son of Amoz came and said to him, 'This is what the LORD says: "Put your affairs in order, for you are about to die; you will not recover."' Then Hezekiah turned his face to the wall and prayed to the LORD, 'Please LORD, remember how I have walked before You faithfully and wholeheartedly and have done what is good in Your sight.' And Hezekiah wept bitterly" (2 Kings 20:1-3).

Zechariah

"The angel said to him: Do not be afraid, Zechariah, because your prayer has been heard. Your wife Elizabeth will bear you a son, and you will name him John" (Luke 1:13).

Answer: 6–b

Day 2 • A Model for Petition

Petition God for your personal needs. Jesus taught this practice to His disciples. In the Model Prayer, after the prayer for God's honor and kingdom, Jesus authorized a series of personal requests.

1. **Read the Model Prayer below. Underline the three personal requests in verses 11-13.**

> ⁹Our Father in heaven,
> Your name be honored as holy.
> ¹⁰Your kingdom come.
> Your will be done
> on earth as it is in heaven.
> ¹¹Give us today our daily bread.
> ¹²And forgive us our debts,
> as we also have forgiven our debtors.
> ¹³And do not bring us into temptation,
> but deliver us from the evil one (Matthew 6:9-13).

Jesus taught us to pray for daily food, forgiveness of sins, and deliverance from temptation and the evil one. These represent three general areas in which God is interested:
• Your physical needs
• Restored fellowship with Him if you have broken it
• Protection from forces beyond your control

Jesus wants you to pray for physical needs. But you are not encouraged to pray for every want or fleshly desire. In fact, too much material wealth can lead you away from God (see Proverbs 30:7-9) if you are not very careful. God knows your needs and considers your motives (see James 4:3). He makes no promises for selfish or greedy requests.

God wants to have intimate fellowship with you. When you sin, the fellowship is broken. Confession of the sin begins the process of restoring this fellowship. You must also seek His forgiveness and turn away from your sin.

Today's Prayer Promise

"When he calls out to Me,
I will answer him;
I will be with him in trouble.
I will rescue him and give
him honor" (Psalm 91:15).

Proverbs 30:7-9

"Two things I ask of You;
don't deny them to me before
I die: Keep falsehood and
deceitful words far from me.
Give me neither poverty nor
wealth; feed me with the
food I need. Otherwise, I
might have too much and
deny You, saying, 'Who is
the LORD?' or I might have
nothing and steal, profaning
the name of my God."

James 4:3

"You ask and don't receive
because you ask wrongly,
so that you may spend it
on your desires for pleasure."

*Temptation** (see Matthew 6:13) can refer to an enticement to sin or to a trial or testing. God promises that He will not allow you to be tested beyond what you can endure (see 1 Corinthians 10:13). He will offer you a way out. You can and should ask God for that deliverance.

Pause and pray these three requests for yourself: physical needs, restored fellowship with God, and protection from evil and temptation.

② Read in the margin the sample prayers of petition. Underline the petitions that would be meaningful for you to pray for yourself or for your group. Write one of your own petitions in the margin below.

Ask for guidance. Jesus Himself practiced the principle of praying for personal needs. Jesus often prayed for guidance. The night before He chose the twelve disciples, Jesus spent the entire night in prayer (see Luke 6:12-13). When the time came to expand His ministry, Jesus arose early in the morning and prayed in "a deserted place" (Mark 1:35). Jesus' prayers demonstrate that divine guidance is available through prayer.

③ Do you have a specific need for God's guidance in an area of your life or work? Describe your need. Then pray for God's guidance.

_____

_____

Ask for wisdom. Another personal petition often found in Scripture is for wisdom. Asking for wisdom is appropriate: "If any of you lacks wisdom, he should ask God, who gives to all generously and without criticizing, and it will be given to him" (James 1:5).

Ask that His will be done. Personal requests should grow from a personal relationship with the Lord. Consider the way God views your personal requests. Think of two personal requests you have made recently or could make today. Prayerfully trace what would happen in the Kingdom or for God's honor if those requests were granted. Learn to say, "Thy Kingdom come in the granting of [specific personal request]." Be alert to ways your Father wants you to become a more godly person.

Close today's lesson with a time of personal petition.

 temptation: an enticement to sin, a trial, testing

1 Corinthians 10:13

"No temptation has overtaken you except what is common to humanity. God is faithful and He will not allow you to be tempted beyond what you are able, but with the temptation He will also provide a way of escape, so that you are able to bear it."

Sample Prayers of Petition

- Heavenly Father, I am Your child.
- Father, I want to be like You. I want to be like Jesus. Teach me to be [name desired characteristics].
- Fill me with Your Holy Spirit.
- Bring glory to Yourself in my body and in my spirit.
- Guide me to know the way I am to go.
- Lord, give me a spirit of wisdom, understanding, knowledge, and reverence for You.

My Petition

Day 3 • Following Your Father's Leading

Scripture-Memory Verse
"Keep asking, and it will be given to you. Keep searching, and you will find. Keep knocking, and the door will be opened to you" (Matthew 7:7).

James 1:17
"Every generous act and every perfect gift is from above, coming down from the Father of lights."

Matthew 7:7-11
"Keep asking, and it will be given to you. Keep searching, and you will find. Keep knocking, and the door will be opened to you. For everyone who asks receives, and the one who searches finds, and to the one who knocks, the door will be opened. What man among you, if his son asks him for bread, will give him a stone? Or if he asks for a fish, will give him a snake? If you then, who are evil, know how to give good gifts to your children, how much more will your Father in heaven give good things to those who ask Him!"

You may not respond to a stranger who delivers a telephone sales pitch. But if you are a parent and the voice in the receiver calls out, "Dad" or "Mom," you will probably make time, even if your schedule is tight. Similarly, God answers prayer because of who you are in relation to Him.

After His resurrection Jesus told Mary Magdalene, "I am ascending to My Father and your Father—to My God and your God" (John 20:17). Can you imagine Mary's feelings when Jesus included her in His family relationship with the Father? In the Model Prayer Jesus also commanded you to pray to God as Father (see Matthew 6:9). You are included too! This relationship between you as a child and your Heavenly Father ought to influence the way you pray. You make your requests of a giving Father.

① **Read in the margin James 1:17 and Matthew 7:7-11. What kind of gifts come down from the Father of heaven?**

_____

② **Which of the following describes the kind of gifts God gives?**
○ a. God gives things that I don't ask for and that will harm me or fail to meet my needs.
○ b. God gives good gifts that will meet my needs. He gives what I ask according to His will.

God is your Heavenly Father, who wants you to develop according to the plans He has for you. He cares what you become. He encourages personal petition to help you become the person He wants you to be. One day you will reign with Christ (see Revelation 5:10 in the right margin). God does not want you to be petty or immature. You are royalty and nobility! Your personal petitions should be directed by the Holy Spirit as He reveals the kind of person you are to become—a witness, a Kingdom worker, a giver, a godly parent or spouse, or one who offers praise to Him in prayer.

When you pray as a child to the Heavenly Father, you should emphasize growing spiritually. You may call Him Father as you talk to Him. Pray to become like Him and like Jesus. Pray for a life that represents the Father well. For His sake pray about maintaining your Father's reputation. Pray for ways to maintain the honor of the family name—Christian—and for characteristics God will develop in you.

③ Read James 3:17 in the margin and underline the character traits (virtues) of godly wisdom. Read Galatians 5:22-23 in the margin and underline the fruit of the Spirit. Read Matthew 5:3-11 in the margin and underline attitudes the Lord blesses.

Here are some virtues God wants to develop in your life and attitudes He blesses. Regularly pray for these traits.[1]

Christlike Virtues (James 3:17)

pure	peace-loving	considerate	submissive
merciful	fruitful	impartial	sincere

Fruit of the Spirit (Galatians 5:22-23)

love	joy	peace	patience	kindness
goodness	faithfulness	gentleness	self-control	

Blessed Attitudes (Matthew 5:3-11)

poor in spirit—dependent on God	merciful—forgiving, caring
mourn—need the Comforter	pure in heart—holy, clean
meek—humble	peacemaker—reconciler
hunger for righteousness	persecuted because of righteousness

Trust, a vital component of a family relationship, is a basis for prayer. On one occasion when some of the Israelites were facing an enemy in battle, "They received help against these enemies, ... because they cried out to God in battle. He granted their request *because they trusted in Him*" (1 Chronicles 5:20, emphasis added). You can trust your Father's leading. What He leads you to become will always be best.

 Pause and pray through the lists of virtues and attitudes you studied today. Ask God to work in you to develop these characteristics. Allow Him to do whatever is necessary to make you the person He wants you to be. The result will always be worth the cost!

Revelation 5:10
"You made them a kingdom and priests to our God, and they will reign on the earth."

James 3:17
"The wisdom from above is first pure, then peace-loving, gentle, compliant, full of mercy and good fruits, without favoritism and hypocrisy."

Galatians 5:22-23
"The fruit of the Spirit is love, joy, peace, patience, kindness, goodness, faith, gentleness, self-control. Against such things there is no law."

Matthew 5:3-11
"Blessed are the poor in spirit. ... Blessed are those who mourn. ... Blessed are the gentle. ... Blessed are those who hunger and thirst for righteousness. ... Blessed are the merciful. ... Blessed are the pure in heart. ... Blessed are the peacemakers. ... Blessed are those who are persecuted for righteousness."

---

1. *The Mind of Christ* by T. W. Hunt and Claude King is a 12-week introduction to a lifelong process of becoming like Christ. God wants to shape you into the image of His Son.

Day 4 • Praying for Yourself

Today's Prayer Promise

"All the things you pray
and ask for—believe that
you have received them,
and you will have them"
(Mark 11:24).

Ask your Heavenly Father
to guide your requests
according to His will
and purposes.

As you learned last week, you can use prayer lists to help you remember to pray for specific concerns. Today you will prepare lists for personal petition.

1. **Prepare lists of personal needs or concerns for which you wish to pray. Use the following categories to stimulate your thinking. Ask your Heavenly Father to guide your requests according to His will and purposes for His kingdom and your life.**

Virtues or attitudes God wants to develop in me: _____

_____

Spiritual needs to be restored to fellowship with my Heavenly Father:

_____

_____

Spiritual needs to be reconciled with fellow Christians: _____

_____

_____

Spiritual growth and maturity: _____

_____

Being a godly family member: _____

_____

_____

Being a faithful church member: _____

_____

Guidance for family, work, church, and ministry: _____

_____

_____

Strength to overcome temptations: _____

_____

Deliverance or protection from _____

_____

Enabling for spiritual ministry: _____

Power and boldness for witness to _____

_____

_____

Emotional needs or concerns: _____

_____

Material or financial needs: _____

_____

Health-and-fitness needs: _____

_____

_____

Work concerns: _____

_____

_____

Others: _____

_____

_____

List here in the margin other personal needs or concerns for which you wish to pray.

Now take time to pray for some of these requests. Emphasize spiritual concerns in your prayers. If you first seek God's kingdom, many of your needs will also be met. Don't hesitate, however, to pray for your human needs. Your Heavenly Father also cares about them.

Today's Prayer Promise

"If any of you lacks wisdom, he should ask God, who gives to all generously and without criticizing, and it will be given to him" (James 1:5).

Romans 15:30

"I implore you, brothers, through the Lord Jesus Christ and through the love of the Spirit, to agonize together with me in your prayers to God on my behalf."

Ephesians 6:19

"Pray also for me, that the message may be given to me when I open my mouth to make known with boldness the mystery of the gospel."

1 Thessalonians 5:25

"Pray for us."

2 Thessalonians 3:1

"Pray for us, brothers, that the Lord's message may spread rapidly and be honored, just as it was with you."

Day 5 • Asking Others to Pray for You

You might ask, Why should I ask someone else to pray for me? Doesn't God hear my prayers? God wants you to ask others to pray for you, and we have biblical reasons to do so. Paul, for example, was convinced that the prayers of other Christians would strengthen his own prayers. Paul asked the churches of his time to pray with him and for him.

① Read the Scriptures in the margin on this page. Underline subjects for which Paul wanted others to pray on his behalf.

② Read the following reasons to ask others to pray for you. Draw stars beside the ones that seem most meaningful to you. Ask God to show you why you need the prayers of others.

ASKING OTHERS TO PRAY FOR YOU

1. *Shows your dependence on God.* God will do some things only in answer to prayer. This way you know that God is the One who provided or acted, and He receives the glory for His actions.
2. *Demonstrates lowliness before God and humility before others.* Pride keeps you from asking others to pray for you. (See 1 Peter 5:5-7 in right margin.)
3. *Brings greater authority to prayer.* God grants greater authority to united prayers of agreement: "If two of you on earth agree about any matter that you pray for, it will be done for you by My Father in heaven" (Matthew 18:19).
4. *Increases the amount of praying in your behalf.* The more persons who pray, the more intercession is made in your behalf.
5. *Broadens the understanding of how to pray for your need.* Others may know exactly how to pray for you even when you don't. They may have been through the same experience. Their specific prayers may secure God's answer for your need.
6. *Blesses those who have the privilege of praying for you.* When people pray for you, they receive a blessing. It is multiplied when they learn that God has answered their prayers. Be sure to give reports of answered prayer to those who are enlisted to pray.
7. *Strengthens the bond of love between you and those who pray for you.* When a person begins to pray intently for another, a bond of love is created or strengthened.
8. *Secures strength for an area of personal weakness or failure.*

WHEN YOU PRAY FOR OTHERS

One need in praying together is praying specific and meaningful prayers. To help focus your prayers, put yourself in the place of the one for whom you are praying so that you can "feel" what she feels. What feelings is she dealing with? Think of problems, conflicts, or pressures the person may face.

If you pray for a person who is grieving over the loss of a spouse, for example, think about the issues the person must deal with. You might pray for the funeral arrangements, the family's travel arrangements, financial needs, loneliness, anger, resentment, bitterness, or a broken heart. You might continue praying about changes the grieving person might confront, reentry into life's routine, or facing holidays. As you mentally place yourself in the circumstances a person faces, you can pray much more specifically, especially if you have faced similar circumstances.

③ **Think about the members of your prayer group and personal concerns they have shared in past weeks. Does one person stand out as someone for whom God wants you to pray? Choose one and write his or her name here: _____**

④ **Try to put yourself in this person's place. List in the margin concerns for which you can pray on this person's behalf.**

You may want to pay attention to specific ways you can be part of the answer to your prayers. As you pray, God may give you a burden to help meet a need. Listen for directions God may give you for meeting the person's needs. These impressions often come only during prayer.

 Close your study today by praying for the person you have chosen. Pray specifically for the needs or concerns you have listed. Ask the Holy Spirit to guide your praying in areas you may not have considered.

SUGGESTIONS FOR PRAYING TOGETHER THIS WEEK

As you pray together, carefully listen for opportunities to respond to others' prayers. If a person makes a personal petition, you might intercede for that need or concern. If a person prays for forgiveness, you might ask the Lord for forgiveness, cleansing, and restoration. If a person asks the Lord a question, be sensitive to the fact that God may speak the answer through you.

1 Peter 5:5-7
"Clothe yourselves with humility toward one another, because God resists the proud, but gives grace to the humble. Humble yourselves therefore under the mighty hand of God, so that He may exalt you in due time, casting all your care upon Him, because He cares about you."

Put yourself in the place of the one for whom you are praying.

Week 6

Intercession

"Confess your sins to one another
and pray for one another, so that you
may be healed. The intense prayer
of the righteous is very powerful."

James 5:16

Intercession

OVERVIEW OF WEEK 6
Day 1: Asking for Others
Day 2: Examples of Intercession
Day 3: Following Your Master's Leading
Day 4: Praying for Others
Day 5: Praying Together in God's Work

VERSE TO MEMORIZE
"Confess your sins to one another and pray for one another, so that you may be healed.
The intense prayer of the righteous is very powerful" (James 5:16).

DISCIPLESHIP HELPS FOR WEEK 6
"Prayers of Intercession" (pp. 102–3)

PREVIEW OF WEEK 6
Intercession is asking for others that is led by your Master. This week you will—
• understand your relationship as a servant to God, your Master;
• learn how to join God's work by seeking and praying for His desires;
• understand why intercession is the greater kind of asking and why a call
  to intercession is one of God's highest callings for a person's life;
• follow biblical models of intercession to pray more effectively for others;
• understand how God works through united prayer to reveal His will and
  purposes to a church or a group;
• discuss what your group will do after this study has ended.

Day 1 • Asking for Others

Intercessory prayer reaches its highest potential when it is intended to further the kingdom of God and to accomplish His will.

Petition is asking for yourself, your family, your church, or your group. Petition is led by your Heavenly Father. A second kind of asking prayer is intercession. Intercession is asking for others that is led by your Master.

1. **What is the second kind of asking prayer?**
   1. Petition   2. _____

God is your Master. You are His servant. God is working to reconcile a lost world to Himself through Christ. He is carrying out His kingdom purposes and has chosen you to be His servant to labor with Him in the kingdom. One way to work with God is through prayers of intercession—praying for others and praying for kingdom purposes to be completed in their lives. God, as your Master, will lead your prayers according to His purposes.

2. **Who leads prayers of intercession?** My _____

AN EXAMPLE OF JESUS' INTERCESSION

Jesus prayed for His disciples. At the Last Supper Jesus told Simon Peter that Satan had asked permission to sift him like wheat. Jesus then told Simon, "I have prayed for you that your faith may not fail. And you, when you have turned back, strengthen your brothers" (Luke 22:32). After Jesus' resurrection and ascension, this prayer made possible Peter's great courage before the Sanhedrin: "When they [the Sanhedrin] observed the boldness of Peter and John and realized that they were uneducated and untrained men, they were amazed and knew that they had been with Jesus" (Acts 4:13; also see vv. 8-12). Intercessory prayer reaches its highest potential when it is intended to further the kingdom of God and to accomplish His will.

THE GREATER KIND OF ASKING

Years ago I (T. W.) began to study all of the prayers of the Bible, especially the asking prayers that were answered with a yes. Eighty of the answered asking prayers in the Bible were personal petition. One hundred thirty-one were intercession. Intercession is the more important kind of asking.

All of God's servants are called to be intercessors.

All of God's servants are called to be intercessors. Some seem to receive a more specific calling to intense intercession. We often call these persons *prayer warriors**—persons who wage spiritual battles in intercessory prayer. The calling to be an intercessor is a high calling.

③ **Have you ever sensed God's calling to a deeper-than-usual role of intercessory prayer?** ○ Yes ○ No

If you answered yes, briefly describe your sense of calling and how you have responded.

_____

_____

④ **Read in the margins today's prayer promise, Romans 8:26-27, as well as Romans 8:34 and Hebrews 7:25. Which two persons of the Trinity intercede for you?**
_____ and _____

Jesus and the Holy Spirit are intercessors for you. When God calls you to be an intercessor, you join Jesus and the Holy Spirit in their work. That is a high calling indeed!

⑤ **How would you rate the importance of being an intercessor?**
○ a. Not very important. Other work is far more important.
○ b. It may be important but only in a crisis.
○ c. Very important—it is also the job of Jesus and the Holy Spirit.

The biblical pattern is that God often did His work through the prayers of great intercessors. When God wanted to deliver the children of Israel from bondage, He raised up Moses to pray for them. When He wanted to deliver them from the murderous plot of Haman, He raised up Esther to fast for them. To rebuild the Jerusalem wall and to renew the covenant, God used the prayers of Nehemiah and Ezra. He started the missionary movement through the prayers of the church in Antioch. The biblical pattern tells us that God does not usually work by Himself. He prefers to work through the prayers of His saints. Intercession is God's basic method for accomplishing His will among people.

↕ **Ask God to train you to be an intercessor. Offer your life to Him for any job of intercession to which He may call you.**

---

prayer warriors—persons who wage spiritual battles in intercessory prayer

Romans 8:34
"Christ Jesus … is at the right hand of God and intercedes for us."

Hebrews 7:25
"He [Jesus] is always able to save those who come to God through Him, since He always lives to intercede for them."

Intercession is God's basic method for accomplishing His will among people.

Day 2 • Examples of Intercession

Intercessory prayer is so important that it can make the difference between life and death. During the early days of the church, King Herod put James to death. Because this pleased the Jews, Herod arrested Peter with the plan to kill him also. "Peter was kept in prison, but prayer was being made earnestly to God for him by the church" (Acts 12:5). In the night an angel of the Lord delivered Peter from prison. Peter immediately went to the house of Mary and John Mark, "where many had assembled and were praying" (Acts 12:12). God worked through the prayers of the early church to spare Peter's life for further service. Your prayers and the prayers of your group could have similar importance in God's kingdom.

1. **Turn to pages 102–3 and read other examples of intercession.**

    a. Who prayed all night? _____

    b. Who wrestled in prayer for God's people? _____

    c. Who prayed for God to forgive those who were killing him?

    _____

    d. What are some of the things Paul prayed for churches?

    _____

    _____

    _____

    _____

Paul's Prayers for Churches

- Knowledge of God's will, spiritual wisdom, and understanding
- Worthy living that would please the Lord
- Spiritual fruit bearing
- Growth in the knowledge of God
- Strength and power
- Endurance, patience, and joy
- Faith, love, and spiritual fullness

Jesus, Epaphras, and Stephen were intercessors. Paul was also a great intercessor who earnestly prayed for churches. Some of the things for which He prayed are listed in the margin.

 Stop and pray some of the following requests for your church or for another church with which you are familiar. Include some of Paul's prayers for the churches. Which request is your greatest burden for God to grant? Circle it.

- Knowledge of God's will, spiritual wisdom, and understanding
- Worthy living that would please the Lord
- Spiritual fruit bearing
- Growth in the knowledge of God
- Strength and power
- Endurance, patience, and joy
- Faith, love, and spiritual fullness

The Bible has many examples of intercessory prayer. You can learn from these examples. Let's examine Jesus' great intercessory prayer in John 17. Concerned about His followers, Jesus prayed for His disciples' spiritual needs. He prayed for them because these would be the leaders in promoting the kingdom of God. For His disciples Jesus requested unity, protection and deliverance, and sanctification or holiness.

(2) **Read in the margin the verses from John 17. On the lines write the verse numbers that relate to each prayer request.**
Unity: _____
Protection and deliverance: _____
Sanctification or holiness: _____

Jesus prayed that His disciples might be one. The great unity He wanted had been disturbed by a quarrel among the disciples about who would be the greatest (see Luke 22:24-27). Jesus asked for that unity four times from four perspectives. He and the disciples had the same power (v. 11), relationship to the Father (v. 21), witness to the world (v. 23), and name (vv. 11-12). Because unity was so significant to Jesus, it ought to be part of your prayers too. Pray for unity not just for one local congregation or one denomination but for all who belong to God through faith in His Son, Jesus.

Jesus also prayed for the disciples' protection, deliverance (vv. 11,15), and sanctification (v. 17). *Sanctified* means *made holy,* and *holy* means *set apart.* No impurity from the world should be allowed into the hearts of God's people, who have been set apart for His work.

 Pray these prayers for your church: for unity, protection, deliverance, and sanctification (being set apart, holy, pure).

Week 6 » Day 2

John 17:11-12,15-23
[11]"Holy Father, protect them by Your name that You have given Me, so that they may be one as We are one. [12]While I was with them, I was protecting them by Your name that You have given Me. [15]I am not praying that You take them out of the world but that You protect them from the evil one. [16]They are not of the world, as I am not of the world. [17]Sanctify them by the truth; Your word is truth. [18]As You sent Me into the world, I also have sent them into the world. [19]I sanctify Myself for them, so they also may be sanctified by the truth. [20]I pray not only for these, but also for those who believe in Me through their message. [21]May they all be one, as You, Father, are in Me and I am in You. May they also be one in Us, so the world may believe You sent Me. [22]I have given them the glory You have given Me. May they be one as We are one. [23]I am in them and You are in Me. May they be made completely one, so the world may know You have sent Me and have loved them as You have loved Me."

Day 3 • Following Your Master's Leading

Scripture-Memory Verse
"Confess your sins to one another and pray for one another, so that you may be healed. The intense prayer of the righteous is very powerful" (James 5:16).

1 Corinthians 7:22-23
"He who is called by the Lord as a slave is the Lord's freedman. Likewise he who is called as a free man is Christ's slave. You were bought at a price; do not become slaves of men."

John 5:17,19-20
"My Father is still working, and I am working also. I assure you: The Son is not able to do anything on His own, but only what He sees the Father doing. For whatever the Father does, the Son also does these things in the same way. For the Father loves the Son and shows Him everything He is doing."

Intercession begins and ends in God.

When Jesus began His earthly ministry, He preached this message: "Repent, because the kingdom of heaven has come near!" (Matthew 4:17). Jesus is the King of this kingdom. The kingdom Jesus spoke of is His rule in the hearts of His people. He is the King, and we are His subjects. He is the Master, and we are His servants (see 1 Corinthians 7:22-23). When you trusted Christ as your Savior, He also became Lord (Master) of your life. As a servant of God, you have tasks to complete that represent His work.

1. **Beside each word indicate whether the role belongs to Christ or to you. Write either a C for *Christ* or an M for *me*.**

    ____ servant   ____ master   ____ subject
    ____ king   ____ lord

Jesus is King, Master, and Lord. You are a servant and a subject. A servant never tells the Master what to do. The Master decides what is important. As God's servant, you join Him in the work He is doing. This was Jesus' approach in knowing and doing His Father's will (see John 5:17,19-20). When you pray as a servant, the emphasis is on God's work. Your objects in prayer are to know the mind and heart of your Master and to pray for His kingdom to come and His will to be done.

2. **Where should your prayer requests originate as you pray for God's kingdom to come and His will to be done?**
    ○ a. I do my best thinking and decide what to ask God to do.
    ○ b. I seek God's direction for my prayer requests.

As your Master, God will lead your intercession. As you pray for others or for Kingdom purposes, seek God's direction for your prayer requests. This may seem strange to you if you have not experienced God's directing your prayers. God is able to give you direction if you are willing to seek it and to wait on Him for an answer.

Servanthood secures God's interest in your prayers for His work. Through the power and authority of the prayers He leads you to pray, God accomplishes His work. Intercession begins and ends in God.

When you pray, you may call Jesus your Master. This will help you keep in mind that He is the One who directs the work of intercession. On the Lord's behalf, pray for the spread of His kingdom and for right relationships with other servants. Pray that His blessings and works will demonstrate His lordship and righteousness.

Your Master will guide your praying according to His will. He has revealed in His Word some of the topics for which He wants you to pray.

③ **Read the verses in the margin. Below each Scripture write the name of someone for whom you can pray.**

The Bible also describes your Master's concerns. As you read and study the Scriptures, you will learn subjects about which to pray. When you read, "The Lord … is patient with you, not wanting any to perish, but all to come to repentance" (2 Peter 3:9), you can pray for God's continued patience and for the salvation of the lost. Micah 6:8 says, "He has told you men what is good and what it is the LORD requires of you: Only to act justly, to love faithfulness, and to walk humbly with your God." Thus, you can pray for justice, faithfulness, and humility. In Isaiah 58:6-7 God reveals actions that please Him:

Isn't the fast I choose:
To break the chains of wickedness,
to untie the ropes of the yoke,
to set the oppressed free,
and to tear off every yoke?
Is it not to share your bread with the hungry,
to bring the poor and homeless into your house,
to clothe the naked when you see him,
and to not ignore your own flesh and blood?

↕ **Approach your Master in prayer. Ask Him to reveal His purposes and to guide your intercession for others. Pray for the persons and concerns you identified in the right margin. Work together with Him as you pray for His kingdom to come and His will to be done on earth as it is in heaven.**

"Pray to the Lord of the harvest to send out workers into His harvest" (Matthew 9:38).

_____

"With every prayer and request, pray at all times in the Spirit, and stay alert in this, with all perseverance and intercession for all the saints" (Ephesians 6:18).

_____

"I urge that petitions, prayers, intercessions, and thanksgivings be made for everyone, for kings and all those who are in authority, so that we may lead a tranquil and quiet life in all godliness and dignity" (1 Timothy 2:1-2).

_____

"Confess your sins to one another and pray for one another, so that you may be healed. The intense prayer of the righteous is very powerful" (James 5:16).

_____

"Love your enemies and pray for those who persecute you" (Matthew 5:44).

_____

Day 4 • Praying for Others

Today's Prayer Promise

"Now to Him who is able to do above and beyond all that we ask or think—according to the power that works in you—to Him be glory in the church and in Christ Jesus to all generations, forever and ever. Amen" (Ephesians 3:20-21).

Possible Requests

- assurance
- bold witnessing
- calling of Christian workers
- Christian fruit
- Christian unity
- conviction of sin
- deliverance
- endurance
- faith
- faithfulness
- filling of the Holy Spirit
- forgiveness
- generosity
- guidance, God's will
- healing—spiritual, emotional, physical
- holiness
- hope
- humility
- integrity
- joy
- judgment
- justice
- knowledge

Instead of learning more about prayer today, you will spend time praying for others. As you learned in week 4, you can use prayer lists to help you remember to pray for specific persons and concerns.

1. **Prepare lists of persons for whom you need to pray, using the following categories to stimulate your thinking. Ask God to bring to mind persons for whom He wants you to intercede.**

   Your family members: _____

   _____

   _____

   Members of your church family: _____

   _____

   _____

   Your pastor and other church leaders: _____

   _____

   _____

   Your coworkers: _____

   _____

   _____

   Relatives, friends, and acquaintances: _____

   _____

   _____

   Other churches and denominations: _____

   _____

   _____

   Missionaries (domestic and international): _____

   _____

   _____

Ministry leaders: _____

_____

_____

Civil authorities (local, regional, and national): _____

_____

_____

Your city, state, province, and nation: _____

_____

_____

Needy or poor persons: _____

_____

_____

Oppressed, abused, or victimized persons: _____

_____

_____

Hungry and homeless persons: _____

_____

_____

Widows, orphans, and prisoners: _____

_____

_____

Sick and homebound persons: _____

_____

_____

Your enemies—those who persecute you: _____

_____

- love
- loyalty
- mercy
- obedience
- patience
- peace
- preservation
- provision of needs
- purity
- reconciliation of broken relationships
- repentance and revival among God's people
- right conduct
- right motives
- spirit of servanthood
- spiritual awakening and conversion of the lost
- spiritual cleansing
- spiritual growth
- stewardship
- surrender and submission to Christ
- understanding
- wisdom

 Take time to pray for some or all persons on your lists. Emphasize spiritual concerns in your prayers. In the margins on the previous pages you will find items you may want to request of the Lord. Try to be specific in your prayers. Take as much time in prayer as possible.

Day 5 • Praying Together in God's Work

Today's Prayer Promise

"I urge that petitions, prayers, intercessions, and thanksgivings be made for everyone, for kings and all those who are in authority, so that we may lead a tranquil and quiet life in all godliness and dignity. This is good, and it pleases God our Savior, who wants everyone to be saved and to come to the knowledge of the truth" (1 Timothy 2:1-4).

My Understanding of God's Will/Purposes

Your church is the body of Christ. Christ is its Head, and every believer is a member of the body. Each member has a function in the body. Think about your physical body for a moment. What would you miss if you had no sight, hearing, smell, touch, or taste? Missing any one of your senses would prevent your body from knowing all it can of the physical world.

In a similar way, all of the members of the body are needed to function where God put them in your church body. If some members are not functioning, your church body is limited in knowing all it can of the spiritual world. As you pray about God's will and purposes, you cannot know God's will for the body without the participation of the other members of your spiritual body. Every contribution adds to your understanding of God's will and of how to pray accordingly.

1. Look back at diagram 6 on page 57. Study the circle in the center. When you pray together with others, you are seeking to understand God's desires. Then you pray in agreement with His will.

Think of God's will for your church as a puzzle. God gives each member one or more pieces. By themselves your pieces may not make sense. But as each piece is shared with the body and put into its place, a beautiful picture begins to become clear. This is why your church needs times to share together and pray together. This would apply as well to committees and the church staff as they seek the Lord's directions for their work.

2. Think about your pieces of a puzzle which represent God's work for your church. In the margin list things you sense God may want to do in or through your church. Before you start writing, let us caution you: this is not a brainstorming session for you to list your ideas. Rather, you need to identify what God has been saying to you. If something comes to mind as you pray through this activity, write it down. As you share these ideas with others, God will either confirm them or not confirm them. Trust that He can and will. Thank Him either way and don't feel offended if an item is not confirmed. All you want is to know your Master's will. Now pray; then consider the following questions as you make your list.

- What burdens has God given you as you have prayed about His will and about your place in His will for your church?
- What needs in your community have you felt a God-given burden to meet?
- What activity in and around your church may indicate an invitation for you to join God's work?
- What scriptural command has God used to convict you about an area your church needs to address (for example, ministry to the poor, needy, oppressed, widows, and orphans or ministries of tithing, loving, witnessing, teaching, and disciple making)?
- Might the kinds of members God has been adding to your body indicate God's preparation for an assignment (for example, medical personnel for medical-missions work, ethnic persons for starting a new church, or construction personnel for building churches in missions areas)?

Have you listed things that you sense God may want to do through your church or prayer group? This may be your part of the message God wants to reveal to your church or group about His will. In your prayer session this week you will have an opportunity to share items on your list. Others will share their lists. Then together you will seek God's perspective on areas He may want you to pray about more completely. This may be a very exciting time as you pray together about God's work in and through your church or group. You may find that God will speak clearly during the prayer time about something special of which He is calling you to be a part.

The early church in the New Testament prayed together about many concerns related to God's will and purposes. They prayed for boldness in witnessing, Christian fruit, the filling of the Spirit, conduct worthy of the Lord, spiritual enlightenment and understanding, deliverance from evil or preservation, the sick, church leaders, missionaries, and persons in authority.

My Church's Understanding of God's Will/Purposes

 Begin praying now for your group prayer time. Ask God to guide your praying according to His will and purposes. Ask Him to speak clearly to your prayer group and to your church about His will and purposes. Don't forget to pray for the larger body of Christ—other churches, denominations, missionaries, and believers in other states, provinces, or countries—that God's kingdom will come and His will be done on earth as it is in heaven. The lines in the right margin are for taking notes during your prayer time with your group.

Week 6 » Day 5

81

Leader Guide

If you have not read the introductory remarks on pages 5–7, do so before continuing.

Pray in Faith is a six-session study in the Growing Disciples Series described on page 112. Although *The Call to Follow Christ* is an introduction to all six disciplines in the series, it is not necessarily a prerequisite. The books in the series can be studied in any sequence; therefore, *Pray in Faith* can follow any of the other studies, or it can serve as a starting place for new and growing believers. Because learning to pray early in the Christian life is so valuable, this may be a good starting place for new believers. New believers, as well as those who have not received much help in prayer and spiritual growth, will benefit most from this course. More mature Christians may find this a valuable refresher course on prayer. You could even use this study to revitalize a midweek prayer service or to begin a church prayer ministry.

Selecting a Leader

Although young believers could study this book together and help one another grow, enlisting a mature believer to lead the group will significantly help the process. Because of the nature of this book's focus on prayer, an experienced intercessor and a small-group prayer leader would be an ideal prospect. Select a leader who has a warm, personal, faithful walk with Christ. Look for good interpersonal skills and the ability to facilitate small-group learning activities.

Small-Group Study

This resource has been designed for a combination of individual and small-group study. In a small group of other believers, Christians can learn from one another, encourage and strengthen one another, and minister to one another. The discipline of prayer is best learned experientially. The body of Christ can function best as members assume responsibility for helping one another grow in Christlikeness. Encourage participants to study the book during the week to learn about and practice the six kinds of prayer. Then they can join other believers in the small group to process and apply what they have learned. Provide a separate group for every 8 to 12 participants so that everyone will be able to participate actively. If you should choose to use this course in a larger group setting like a midweek prayer service, plan to divide into smaller groups of 8 to 12 for prayer and sharing times. Members will need to be active participants rather than silent observers.

One-to-One Mentoring

If circumstances prevent your studying this book in a small-group setting in which you have access to a variety of spiritual gifts, you may choose to use it in a one-to-one mentoring process. To do so, study the devotionals each day and meet at least once each week to discuss what you are learning and to spend time praying together. Use the following session plans to get ideas for your personal discussions and prayer time.

Order Books

Each participant will need a copy of this book. Each spouse in a couple will want his or her own book to respond to learning activities and prepare a prayer journal. To order additional copies of this resource, write to LifeWay Church Resources Customer Service; One LifeWay Plaza; Nashville, TN 37234-0113; fax order to (615) 251-5933; phone toll free (800) 458-2772; order online at *www.lifeway.com;* e-mail *orderentry@ lifeway.com;* or visit the LifeWay Christian Store serving you.

Enlisting Participants

Scan the list below and check one or more possible groups with which you could begin praying together.

○ New Christians
○ Discipleship group
○ Multiethnic group
○ Prayer group
○ Coworkers
○ Prayer partners
○ Senior-adult group
○ Men's group
○ Your children
○ Your spouse
○ Youth group
○ Prison or jail inmates
○ Midweek prayer service
○ Interdenominational prayer group
○ Prayer-ministry participants
○ Citywide prayer meeting

○ Church staff
○ Missions group
○ Neighbors
○ Committee/board
○ Fellow pastors
○ Elders or deacons
○ Family members
○ Women's group
○ Friends
○ Group of teachers
○ Home cell group

As you enlist participants, give members a book before the first session and ask them to study the introduction and week 1 prior to the meeting. Include other more mature believers in the group so that each subgroup will include someone who will be comfortable praying for the others and who can lead in discussion and prayer.

Your Role as the Leader

You are not required to be a content expert to teach this course. Participants study the content during the week. Your role is to facilitate group discussion, sharing, and praying to process and apply what participants have learned during the week. Be sensitive to the spiritual growth of members and pay special attention to those who may struggle along the way. Don't hesitate to enlist the help of more mature believers in the group to help you nurture the others and to help facilitate prayer times.

Time and Schedule

This course is designed for six sessions. Each group session needs to follow the study of the corresponding week's daily devotions. Members will need to have books so that they can study the first week's material prior to the first session. Allow at least one hour for each session. Some groups may prefer longer sessions to accommodate more sharing and more prayer time.

Optional Introductory Session

You may prefer to start with an introductory session so that you can overview the study, distribute books, get acquainted, and make assignments for the first week. To do so, draw a chart and introduce the six kinds of prayer (p. 5). Use the Discipleship Helps on pages 92–103 to give examples of each type of prayer. In your own words tell the story of the calls to united prayer (pp. 6–7). Explain that your small-group experiences will primarily be prayer times in which you will practice what you learn during the week. Describe the process you will follow of combining individual study and small-group discussion and prayer.

Encouraging Reluctant Pray-ers

Because you may have a number of participants who are hesitant to pray aloud, you may want to encourage them in the following ways.

- Give them permission not to pray aloud if they are not ready to do so.
- Promise that you will not call on them to pray or pray around the circle and put them on the spot. Always ask for volunteers unless you know the person is comfortable praying aloud.
- Remind them that they will learn and practice prayer during the week and will then practice in the small group what they have learned on their own.
- State that prayer is conversation with God and not a formal, technical language. They do not have to master a special language to converse with God.

Preparing to Lead the Sessions

Make prayer a major part of your preparation throughout the course. God will work and guide in answer to prayer, and you will model the discipline of prayer in the process. Leading the small-group sessions should not require large amounts of time in advance preparation. However, you will benefit by studying the suggestions on the following pages. Use these as options, not as a rigid structure to follow. Allow the needs of your group to dictate the way you use your discussion and prayer time each week. Decide which activities and questions to use in your study and determine approximate times for transitions between segments. Select activities that are most appropriate for your group's maturity level. Our prayer is that by the end of your study, your group may be so experienced praying together that the Holy Spirit will be the only Guide you will need!

Provide name tags for the first few sessions so that members can easily learn names.

Leading the Session

Guide group members to share responses or to pray, following the plans you have prepared. You may want to divide the group into smaller groups of three to five for some of the prayer times. If needed, invite members to turn to the session-plans page and follow the instructions for sharing or praying. Be sensitive to needs that may arise during sharing times that call for immediate prayer.

Session 1 • Six Kinds of Prayer

Opening Prayer

Read Luke 11:1-13. Acknowledge the Lord's presence with you. Ask the Lord to teach you to pray during the coming weeks. Ask Him to encourage your persistence in prayer and ask Him to fill each of you with His Holy Spirit.

Getting Acquainted

Write members' names on the inside back cover of your book. Share the following to introduce yourself:

1. Name and information about your immediate family
2. Where do you spend most of your waking hours during the week (business or work, home, school, etc.)?
3. Why did you decide to participate in this study?

Reviewing Week 1 and Sharing Responses

1. What is the difference between prayer as a religious activity and prayer as a relationship with God? Discuss. (pp. 10–11)
2. What are two groups of prayers we will study, and what is the purpose of each? Which group is more focused on being, and which one is focused on doing? (pp. 12–13)
3. What are four types of responding prayers, and to what aspect of God's nature do you respond in each type? (pp. 14–15)
4. What are two types of asking prayers, and who leads your praying in each? (pp. 16–17)

This Week's Prayer Focus: Confession

(See pages 92–93 for examples and topics.)

1. Allow for a quiet time in which members pray privately to prepare themselves to enter the group prayer time.
2. Use these and other subjects for confession:
   • Confess truths about God and about your relationship with Him.
   • Confess your needs, the needs of others, and the needs of your church.
   • Confess the truths of your new nature in Christ.

Interacting with the Scriptures

1. Invite a volunteer to quote Matthew 21:22. Encourage members to memorize a Scripture verse each week.
2. What verse or passage of Scripture has been most meaningful or challenging to you this week and why?

Praying Together

Turn to page 19, activity 4. What suggestions for praying together do you believe will be most helpful for our group to practice and why? Now apply these suggestions in prayer. Begin with responding prayers. As time permits, pray the requests mentioned.

Previewing Week 2

Use the overview on page 21 to preview your study for the coming week.

Closing Prayer

Pray for the group and ask the Lord to teach each person to pray more effectively.

Opening Prayer

Instead of a single prayer, use the following suggestions for this week's prayer focus on praise and spend an extended time in praise to the Lord. Encourage members to try to refrain from making requests during this time. (We know that's hard; just try.)

This Week's Prayer Focus: Praise

(See pages 94–95 for examples and topics.) Invite group members to praise God for who He is. Ask them to make statements of praise to God, focusing on one or more attributes. They may want to read Scriptures of praise or to quote a line of praise from a hymn. After each statement of praise, ask members to quote together these phrases from Psalm 67:3: "Let the people praise thee, O God; let all the people praise thee" (KJV)—like a soloist with a choir backup singing the chorus.

Reviewing Week 2 and Sharing Responses

1. Using a marker board, see if you can list all 10 reasons to pray. For which reasons do you sense a need to pray most and why? As people share, listen for opportunities to pause and pray for a need that may be expressed. When appropriate, ask a volunteer to pray. (p. 23)
2. What does "pray constantly" mean? (p. 24)
3. How different was your day when you tried to remain in an attitude of prayer throughout the day? (p. 25, activity 3)
4. What are five ways to use Scripture in prayer? Give an example of each one. Which ones have been meaningful to you? (p. 29)

5. Share your responses to activity 2 and explain why. (p. 30)
6. How important is unity as we pray together? (p. 31)

Interacting with the Scriptures

1. Invite a volunteer to quote Matthew 18:19.
2. What verse, prayer promise, or other Scripture has been most meaningful or challenging to you this week and why?
3. What truth about prayer has been most meaningful or practical this week?

Praying Together

You may want to divide into smaller groups of three to five for the following prayer time. Invite members to turn to their prayer lists on pages 104–9. Practice praying about one subject at a time. One member will pray a prayer about one of her requests. Then others will join in praying about that concern. After several have prayed, another member will pray about one of his requests, and the group will join him in prayer.

As a larger group, pray that God will develop your church into a house of prayer for the nations. Pray for unity.

Previewing Week 3

Use the overview on page 33 to preview your study for the coming week.

Closing Prayer

Close by reciting (or reading) in unison the Model Prayer (Matthew 6:9-13; see p. 30).

Session 3 • Responding Prayers

Because this week's prayer session focuses on responding prayers, plan to spend extra time in confession, praise, worship, and thanksgiving. However, if group members' needs or other concerns warrant more time in asking prayers, follow the Holy Spirit's leadership. Use these suggestions only as a guide. As you develop confidence praying together, you may wish to depend less on these suggestions, allowing the Holy Spirit to direct your prayer time.

Opening Prayer
Use the following suggestions to begin this session with prayers of worship.

This Week's Prayer Focus: Worship
(See pages 96–97 for examples and topics.) Using Scriptures and the sample prayers, worship the Lord and express to Him your awe, admiration, and love.

Reviewing Week 3 and Sharing Responses
1. Name and describe four kinds of responding prayers. Explain how these prayers can help you become more like the Lord.
2. What is the difference between God's attributes and His glory? Give examples of each. (p. 36–39)
3. What are some ways to express prayers of worship? (p. 38–39)
4. What are some ways God has blessed us with spiritual blessings? (p. 40, activity 2)
5. Read and discuss the guidelines for the confession of sin. (pp. 42–43)

Interacting with the Scriptures
1. Invite a volunteer to quote Hebrews 13:15.
2. What verse, prayer promise, or other Scripture has been most meaningful or challenging to you this week and why?
3. What truth about prayer has been most meaningful or practical this week?

Praying Together
1. Divide into same-gender groups of four or five. Begin by confessing the truth. Offer time for individuals to confess sin that needs public confession or for which they need strength for victory. Confess sins to one another, following the guidelines on pages 42–43.
2. Use the helps on pages 94–99 to praise and worship the Lord and give Him thanks. Don't rush. Enjoy this time with the Lord.
3. As time permits, pray for each other to grow strong in the Lord.

Previewing Week 4
Use the overview on page 45 to preview your study for the coming week.

Closing Prayer
Invite members to join hands. Call on one person to read the following benediction from Jude 24-25: "To Him who is able to protect you from stumbling and to make you stand in the presence of His glory, blameless and with great joy, to the only God our Savior, through Jesus Christ our Lord, be glory, majesty, power, and authority before all time, now, and forever. Amen."

Session 4 • Asking Prayers

Opening Prayer

Invite volunteers to pray sentence prayers of praise and worship as you begin the session.

Reviewing Week 4 and Sharing Responses

1. What are eight reasons God answers prayer? Which one of these stands out as particularly meaningful or practical to you and why? (pp. 48–49)
2. Ask volunteers: What prayer request did you list, and what did you identify as reasons God would want to answer it? (p. 49)
3. What are some reasons God does not answer prayer or says no? (pp. 50–51)
4. In your opinion which of these reasons may be the greatest cause of unanswered prayer in the church today and why?
5. Without looking, see if you can identify the 10 principles for asking. (pp. 52–53)
6. Using the diagrams (or draw them on a marker board), describe what praying in agreement means. (pp. 54–57)

This Week's Prayer Focus: Thanksgiving

(See pages 98–99 for examples and topics.)

1. What are some ways God has bestowed His blessings, riches, and bounty on you? Tell of specific times or ways God has blessed or provided.
2. Take turns giving thanks and expressing your gratitude to the Lord for what He has done.

Interacting with the Scriptures

1. Invite a volunteer to quote Philippians 4:6.
2. What verse, prayer promise, or other Scripture has been most meaningful or challenging to you this week and why?
3. What truth about prayer or experience with God in prayer has been most meaningful or practical this week?

Praying Together

Divide into same-gender groups of four or five. Explain that group members will pray for one another. This is not a time to pray for others for whom you are concerned but for you. Addressing one person at a time, ask: How may we pray for you? After a person shares, spend a few minutes praying for him or her. More than one person can pray. After you've prayed for one person, move to the next person and follow the same process until everyone has been prayed for.

Previewing Week 5

Use the overview on page 59 to preview your study for the coming week.

Closing Prayer

Pray that the Lord will teach participants by experience how to pray in agreement with Him and with one another. Thank Him for His presence with you as you pray together.

Session 5 • Petition

Opening Prayer

Invite volunteers to pray sentence prayers of confession, praise, worship, and thanksgiving as you begin.

Invite volunteers to share testimonies of what God is doing to develop their prayer lives or ways He has answered prayers in a meaningful way.

Reviewing Week 5 and Sharing Responses

1. Which area do you most need to work on so that you can pray in agreement with God? (p. 60, activity 5)
2. Why does God encourage you to ask for yourself? (p. 61)
3. What are three general areas in which Jesus encouraged prayer for yourself? (p. 62)
4. What are some of the virtues, fruit, or attitudes God wants to develop in you and about which you can pray? (p. 65)
5. What are some reasons to ask others to pray for you? Which of these have you experienced during the past few weeks and how? (p. 68)
6. What are some ways you can respond to the prayers of others as you pray together? Discuss examples. Pay special attention this week to responding to others' prayers. (p. 69)

Interacting with the Scriptures

1. Invite a volunteer to quote Matthew 7:7.
2. What verse, prayer promise, or other Scripture has been most meaningful or challenging to you this week and why?

3. What truth about prayer or experience with God in prayer has been most meaningful or practical this week?

This Week's Prayer Focus: Petition and Praying Together

(See pages 100–101 for examples and topics.) Spend a greater portion of your prayer time focusing on petition. Encourage members to request prayer for personal needs or concerns. Rather than state a request to the group, participants may choose to pray for their own needs or concerns. As one prays for a personal concern, encourage the rest of the group to respond to the prayer and to join in intercession. You may find that the personal concerns lead you to intercession for related persons or concerns. Give the Holy Spirit great freedom to guide your praying during this session.

Reflection (five min.)

Explain that the purpose of the reflection time is not to criticize others but to help one another learn more effective ways to pray together. Use the questions on page 110 to assess the effectiveness of your prayer time. Record any suggestions for improving.

Previewing Week 6

Use the overview on page 71 to preview your study for the coming week.

Closing Prayer

Summarize what you sense God has done during your prayer time. Ask Him to make your church a house of prayer for the nations.

Session 6 • Intercession

Opening Prayer
Invite a volunteer to pray for your group and for this closing session.

Reviewing Week 6 and Sharing Responses
1. What is a prayer warrior? Do you know anyone like that? Whom? (p. 73)
2. What are some of your greatest prayer burdens for your church? (pp. 74–75)
3. As you have prayed for others, has God given you a special burden for one person or group? If so, whom? (pp. 78–79)

This Week's Prayer Focus: Intercession
(See pages 102–3 for examples and topics.) Focus on praying for others who are not part of your group. Consider some of these:
• Broken, hurting persons in the news
• Single parents
• Persons in nursing homes
• Sick and homebound persons
• Missionaries at home or overseas
• Missionaries at home
• People in war-torn areas of the world
• Refugees
• Christian ministries
• Prisoners (lost and Christian)
• Other churches
• The homeless, poor, and oppressed
• Orphans and widows
• Persons who are grieving
• Government leaders, military personnel

Interacting with the Scriptures
1. Invite a volunteer to quote James 5:16.

2. What verse, prayer promise, or other Scripture has been most meaningful or challenging to you this week and why?
3. What truth about prayer has been most meaningful or practical this week?

Praying Together
Encourage members to share from pages 80–81 what they sense to be God's will and purposes for your church. Explain that this is part of praying together. Members need to hear from one another and from the Lord through others. Listen to learn whether several members mention similar or identical concerns. These may indicate directions in which to focus your praying. Pray for God's purposes as He leads your praying. Pray for one subject at a time.

What's Next?
What do you sense that God wants us to do next to continue becoming a house of prayer? Consider these:
1. Continue meeting monthly, weekly, or daily for concentrated periods of praying.
2. Study *Disciple's Prayer Life* by T. W. Hunt and Catherine Walker to go much deeper in our practice of personal prayer.
3. Study *A House of Prayer: Prayer Ministries in Your Church* and pray about other types of prayer ministry for your church.

Closing Prayer
Invite volunteers to pray prayers of thanksgiving for what God has taught you, what He has done in your group, and the ways He's answered prayers over the past six weeks.

Six Kinds of Prayer

PRAYER	NATURE OF THE PRAYER	GOD
Confession	Responding to …	God's holiness
Praise	Responding to …	God's attributes
Worship	Responding to …	God's glory
Thanksgiving	Responding to …	God's riches
Petition	Asking that is led by …	Your Heavenly Father
Intercession	Asking that is led by …	Your Master

Confession means agreeing with God. Confession includes agreeing with God about the nature of your sin, after which you seek God's cleansing and restoration to intimate fellowship. Confession is a good beginning place for prayer, preparing you to enter the presence of Holy God.

Praise is lifting up the attributes of God. You have a tendency to become like what you value or praise. By lifting up God's attributes in praise, you respond to Him by becoming more like Him. Through praise you elevate Him in the eyes and ears of others.

Worship: When God reveals His Person and His glory, you love Him and long to be with Him. You respond to God's glory through prayers of worship. You worship by expressing your awe, reverence, honor, love, and adoration for God.

Thanksgiving is responding to God's riches bestowed through His blessings. Thanksgiving is not just an act or a statement. It is an attitude of gratitude. Prayers of thanksgiving reveal a relationship between the Giver and the receiver.

Petition: God is your Heavenly Father. He wants you to show the world what a child of God looks like. Therefore, He will guide your petitions to help you become more like Him.

Intercession: God is Master, and you are His Servant. God has chosen you to labor with Him through prayers of intercession. Intercessory prayers are for God's kingdom purposes to be completed in the lives of others. Your Master will lead you to pray for His purposes.

Prayers of Confession

(See pp. 34–35.) When you enter God's presence, you become aware of His holiness. In the presence of God's holiness you become aware of your sinfulness. Sin hinders your prayer relationship with God. *Confession* means *agreeing with God.* Confession includes agreeing with God about the nature of your sin, after which you seek God's cleansing and restoration to intimate fellowship. Confession is a good beginning place for prayer, preparing you to enter the presence of Holy God.

Confession is also agreeing with God about the truth. You can confess who God is. You can agree with Him about who you are in relationship to Him. You can agree with Him about the truth of your circumstances or your need.

Examples of Confession of Sin

"[David] said to the LORD, 'I have sinned greatly in what I've done. Now, LORD, because I've been very foolish, please take away your servant's guilt'" (2 Samuel 24:10).

"Our iniquities are higher than our heads and our guilt is as high as the heavens. Our guilt has been terrible from the days of our fathers until the present. Now, our God, what can we say in light of this? For we have abandoned the commandments you gave through Your servants the prophets. LORD God of Israel, You are righteous. … Here we are before You with our guilt, though no one can stand in Your presence because of this" (Ezra 9:6-7,10-11,15).

"Be gracious to me, God,
according to Your faithful love;
according to Your abundant compassion,
blot out my rebellion.
Wash away my guilt,
and cleanse me from my sin.
For I am conscious of my rebellion,
and my sin is always before me.
Against You—You alone—I have sinned
and done this evil in Your sight.
So You are right when You pass sentence;
You are blameless when You judge.
Purify me with hyssop, and I will be clean;
wash me, and I will be whiter than snow.
Let me hear joy and gladness;
let the bones You have crushed rejoice.
Turn Your face away from my sins
and blot out all my guilt.
God, create a clean heart for me
and renew a steadfast spirit within me.
Do not banish me from Your presence
or take Your Holy Spirit from me.
Restore the joy of Your salvation to me,
and give me a willing spirit.
Then I will teach the rebellious Your ways,
and sinners will return to You"
(Psalm 51:1-4,7-13).

"Though our guilt testifies against us,
LORD, act for Your name's sake.
Indeed, our rebellions are many;
we have sinned against You" (Jeremiah 14:7).

"Forgive us our debts,
as we also have forgiven our debtors"
(Matthew 6:12).

Group Confession

"Those of Israelite descent separated them-selves from all foreigners, and they stood and confessed their sins and the guilt of their fathers. While they stood in their places, they read from the book of the law of the LORD their God for a fourth of the day and spent another fourth of the day in confession and worship of the LORD their God" (Nehemiah 9:2-3).

Promise for Confession

"If we confess our sins, He is faithful and righteous to forgive us our sins and to cleanse us from all unrighteousness" (1 John 1:9).

Examples of Confession of Truth

"Simon Peter answered, 'You are the Messiah, the Son of the living God!'" (Matthew 16:16).

"Master, You are the One who made the heaven, the earth, and the sea, and every-thing in them" (Acts 4:24).

_____

_____

_____

_____

_____

_____

Sample Prayers of the Confession of Truth

- Sin no longer has dominion over me.
- You have dressed me in robes of Your righteousness.
- You are Lord and Master; I am Your servant.
- You are my Father; I am Your child.
- You are Sovereign; my answer is yes.
- You are Truth; You are my Way and Life.
- I walk in victory with Christ.
- Greater is He who is in me than he who is in the world.

_____

_____

_____

_____

_____

_____

_____

_____

_____

Prayers of Praise

(See pp. 36–37.) In many different ways God reveals to you what He is like. His character traits are called His attributes. Praise is lifting up the attributes of God. You have a tendency to become like what you value or praise. By lifting up God's attributes in praise, you respond to Him by becoming more like Him. Through praise you elevate Him in the eyes and ears of others.

Examples of Praise

"I will praise you, O Lord, with all my heart;
    I will tell of all your wonders.
I will be glad and rejoice in you;
    I will sing praise to your name,
    O Most High" (Psalm 9:1-2, NIV).

"Your name, God, like Your praise,
    reaches to the ends of the earth;
Your right hand is filled with justice"
(Psalm 48:10).

"I will praise You, Lord, among the peoples;
I will sing praises to You among the nations.
For Your faithful love is as high
    as the heavens;
Your faithfulness reaches to the clouds"
(Psalm 57:9-10).

"My lips will glorify You
    because Your faithful love is better than life"
(Psalm 63:3).

"You are my God, and I will give You thanks.
You are my God; I will exalt You"
(Psalm 118:28).

"I praise You seven times a day
    for Your righteous judgments" (Psalm 119:164).

"I will give You thanks with all my heart;
I will sing Your praise before the heavenly beings.
I will bow down toward Your holy temple
    and give thanks to Your name
for Your constant love and faithfulness.
You have exalted Your name
    and Your promise above everything else"
(Psalm 138:1-2).

"I will praise You,
    because I have been remarkably
        and wonderfully made.
Your works are wonderful,
    and I know this very well" (Psalm 139:14).

"Yahweh is great and is highly praised;
His greatness is unsearchable.
One generation will declare Your works
    to the next
and will proclaim Your mighty acts.
I will speak of Your glorious splendor
and Your wonderful works" (Psalm 145:3-5).

Mary's Praise

"My soul proclaims the greatness of the Lord,
and my spirit has rejoiced in God my Savior,
because the Mighty One
has done great things for me,
and His name is holy.
His mercy is from generation to generation
on those who fear Him.
He has done a mighty deed with His arm"
(Luke 1:46-47,49-51).

Praise Commended

"Hallelujah!
How good it is to sing to our God,
for praise is pleasant and lovely"
(Psalm 147:1).

"Praise God in His sanctuary.
Praise Him in His mighty heavens.
Praise Him for His powerful acts;
praise Him for His abundant greatness.
Praise Him with trumpet blast;
praise Him with harp and lyre.
Praise Him with tambourine and dance;
praise Him with flute and strings.
Praise Him with resounding cymbals;
praise Him with clashing cymbals.
Let everything that breathes praise the LORD."
(Psalm 150).

"Give thanks to the LORD; proclaim His name!
Celebrate His deeds among the peoples.
Declare that His name is exalted" (Isaiah 12:4).

"Through Him [Jesus] let us continually
offer up to God a sacrifice of praise, that is,
the fruit of our lips that confess His name"
(Hebrews 13:15).

Biblical Words for Praise

praise	hallelujah	alleluia
hosanna	magnify	exalt
rejoice	exult	ascribe
bless	laud	worship
adore	honor	glorify

Attributes of God

able	almighty	all-knowing
attentive	awesome	all-powerful
beautiful	blameless	compassionate
blessed	enthroned	ever present
eternal	exalted	has authority
faithful	first	has integrity
flawless	forgiving	gentle
glorious	good	gracious
healing	holy	indescribable
invisible	jealous	just
kind	last	light
living	majestic	merciful
mighty	patient	peaceful
perfect	protective	pure
radiant	righteous	slow to anger
spirit	strong	supreme
sure	tender	understanding
true	unique	unfailing love
wise	wonderful	abounding love

_____

_____

_____

_____

_____

_____

_____

_____

_____

_____

_____

Prayers of Worship

(See pp. 38–39.) God has acted in history, including your history. Because of His nature (attributes), God's actions reveal His glory—His beauty, His splendor, and His worth. God's glory is the evidence of His attributes. For instance, you know that God is powerful (an attribute). When God shows His power by giving you victory in a situation, He reveals His glory. The same is true when God reveals His love, mercy, forgiveness, justice, and other qualities. When God reveals His Person this way, you love Him and long to be with Him. You respond to God's glory through prayers of worship. You worship by expressing your reverence, honor, love, and adoration for God.

Examples of Worship

"Yours, LORD, is the greatness and the power and the glory and the splendor and the majesty, for everything in the heavens and on earth belongs to You. Yours, LORD, is the kingdom, and You are exalted as head over all. Riches and honor come from You, and You are the ruler of everything. In Your hand are power and might, and it is in Your hand to make great and to give strength to all" (1 Chronicles 29:11-12).

"As a deer longs for streams of water, so I long for You, God. I thirst for God, the living God" (Psalm 42:1-2).

"All the nations You have made will come and bow down before You, Lord, and will honor Your name. For You are great and perform wonders; You alone are God" (Psalm 86:9-10).

"Our Lord and God, You are worthy to receive glory and honor and power, because You have created all things, and because of Your will they exist and were created" (Revelation 4:11).

"You are worthy to take the scroll and to open its seals; because You were slaughtered, and You redeemed people for God by Your blood from every tribe and language and people and nation. They said with a loud voice: The Lamb who was slaughtered is worthy to receive power and riches and wisdom and strength and honor and glory and blessing!" (Revelation 5:9,12).

"Great and awe-inspiring are Your works, Lord God, the Almighty; righteous and true are Your ways, King of the Nations. Lord, who will not fear and glorify Your name? Because You alone are holy, because all the nations will come and worship before You, because Your righteous acts have been revealed" (Revelation 15:3-4).

Worship Commended

"Give the LORD—you heavenly beings—
give the LORD glory and strength.
Give the LORD the glory due His name;
worship the LORD
in the splendor of His holiness" (Psalm 29:1-2).

"Come, let us worship and bow down;
let us kneel before the LORD our Maker"
(Psalm 95:6).

"Serve the LORD with gladness;
come before Him with joyful songs"
(Psalm 100:2).

"Let us go to His dwelling place;
let us worship at His footstool" (Psalm 132:7).

Expressing Prayers of Worship

1. Describe your reverence for God.
2. Magnify the Lord.
3. Exalt the Lord.
4. Ascribe to the Lord the glory due Him.
5. Bless the Lord.
6. Glorify the Lord.

_____

_____

_____

_____

_____

_____

Sample Prayers of Worship

- I bless You, Lord.
- Honor and majesty belong to You.
- I stand in awe of Your greatness and power.
- I love You because You first loved me.
- I long to be with You, Lord. I hunger and thirst for You.
- I would rather be a doorkeeper in Your house than live as a rich person with the wicked.
- I glorify Your name because You have done great things.
- The heavens declare Your glory, Lord. I worship You in the splendor of Your holiness.
- The earth is full of Your glory, Lord. Your wisdom, knowledge, and power are beyond my understanding.
- Lord, Your splendor and majesty are glorious. I worship You.
- I long to be with You in eternity. I yearn for my redemption to be complete in Christ.
- I desire intimate fellowship with You.

_____

_____

_____

_____

_____

Prayers of Thanksgiving

(See pp. 40–41.) God is our source for abundant living. He bestows on us material and spiritual blessings according to His grace. When God reveals Himself by giving blessings to you, thanksgiving is a natural response. Thanksgiving is responding to God's riches bestowed through His blessings. Thanksgiving is not just an act or a statement. It is an attitude of gratitude. Prayers of thanksgiving reveal a relationship between the Giver and the receiver.

Examples of Thanksgiving

"Riches and honor come from You, and You are the ruler of everything. In Your hand are power and might, and it is in Your hand to make great and to give strength to all. Now therefore, our God, we give You thanks and praise Your glorious name"
(1 Chronicles 29:12-13).

"You turned my lament into dancing;
You removed my sackcloth
and clothed me with gladness,
so that I can sing to You and not be silent.
LORD my God, I will praise You forever"
(Psalm 30:11-12).

"We give thanks to You, God;
we give thanks to You, for Your name is near.
People tell about Your wonderful works"
(Psalm 75:1).

"LORD, I am indeed Your servant;
I am Your servant, the son of Your
  female servant.
You have loosened my bonds.
I will offer You a sacrifice of thanksgiving
  and will worship the LORD" (Psalm 116:16-17).

"We thank You, Lord God, the Almighty,
  who is and who was,
  because You have taken Your great power
  and have begun to reign" (Revelation 11:17).

Daniel's Prayers of Thanksgiving

"I offer thanks and praise to You,
  God of my fathers,
  because You have given me
  wisdom and power.
And now You have let me know
  what we asked of You,
  for You have let us know
  the king's mystery" (Daniel 2:23).

Jesus' Prayers of Thanksgiving

"I praise You, Father, Lord of heaven and earth, because You have hidden these things from the wise and learned and revealed them to infants" (Matthew 11:25).

"Jesus took the loaves, and after giving thanks He distributed them to those who were seated—so also with the fish, as much as they wanted" (John 6:11).

"Jesus raised His eyes and said, 'Father, I thank You that You heard Me'" (John 11:41).

Paul's Prayers of Thanksgiving

"I never stop giving thanks for you as I remember you in my prayers" (Ephesians 1:16).

"I give thanks to Christ Jesus our Lord, who has strengthened me, because He considered me faithful, appointing me to the ministry" (1 Timothy 1:12).

A Call to Thanksgiving

"Give thanks to the LORD, call on His name; proclaim His deeds among the peoples" (Psalm 105:1).

"Give thanks to the LORD, for He is good; His faithful love endures forever" (Psalm 107:1).

"Don't worry about anything, but in everything, through prayer and petition with thanksgiving, let your requests be made known to God" (Philippians 4:6).

"Give thanks in everything, for this is God's will for you in Christ Jesus" (1 Thessalonians 5:18).

Subjects for Thanks
• Redemption, mercy, grace, forgiveness
• Meaningful spiritual experiences
• Family, relatives, friends, and church
• Provision for your needs
• Persons and events that have had spiritual impacts on your life

_____

_____

_____

_____

Prayers of Petition

(See week 5.) God is your Heavenly Father. Through you He wants you to show the world what a child of God looks like. Therefore, He will guide your petitions. Through these prayers you will work with God as He helps you become more like Him.

Examples of Petition

"Give Your servant an obedient heart to judge Your people and to discern between good and evil. For who is able to judge this great people of Yours?" (1 Kings 3:9).

"At the time for offering the evening sacrifice, Elijah the prophet approached the altar and said, 'LORD God of Abraham, Isaac, and Israel, today let it be known that You are God in Israel and I am Your servant, and that at Your word I have done all these things. Answer me, LORD! Answer me so that this people will know that You, Yahweh, are God and that You have turned their hearts back'" (1 Kings 18:36-37).

"If only You would bless me, extend my border, let Your hand be with me, and keep me from harm, so that I will not cause any pain" (1 Chronicles 4:10).

"Please, Lord, let Your ear be attentive to the prayer of Your servant and to that of Your servants who delight to revere Your name. Give Your servant success today, and have compassion on him in the presence of this man" (Nehemiah 1:11).

"They were all trying to intimidate us. ... 'But now, my God, strengthen me'" (Nehemiah 6:9).

"My Father! If it is possible, let this cup pass from Me. Yet not as I will, but as You will" (Matthew 26:39).

"I do believe! Help my unbelief" (Mark 9:24).

Petitions from Psalms

"Answer me when I call,
God, who vindicates me.
You freed me from affliction;
be gracious to me and hear my prayer"
(Psalm 4:1).

"LORD, do not rebuke me in Your anger;
do not discipline me in Your wrath"
(Psalm 6:1).

"LORD my God, I seek refuge in You;
save me from all my pursuers and rescue me"
(Psalm 7:1).

"LORD, I turn my hope to You.
My God, I trust in You.
Do not let me be disgraced;
do not let my enemies gloat over me"
(Psalm 25:1-2).

"God, hear my cry;
pay attention to my prayer.
I call to You from the ends of the earth
when my heart is without strength.

Lead me to a rock that is high above me"
(Psalm 61:1-2).

"God, deliver me.
Hurry to help me, LORD!" (Psalm 70:1).

"Teach me Your way, LORD,
and I will live by Your truth.
Give me an undivided mind to fear
Your name" (Psalm 86:11).

"Search me, God, and know my heart;
test me and know my concerns.
See if there is any offensive way in me;
lead me in the everlasting way"
(Psalm 139:23-24).

"Let me experience
Your faithful love in the morning,
for I trust in You.
Reveal to me the way I should go,
because I long for You" (Psalm 143:8).

Sample Prayers of Petition

• Heavenly Father, I am Your child.
• Father, I want to be like You. I want to be
  like Jesus. Teach me to be [name desired
  characteristics].
• Fill me with Your Holy Spirit.
• Bring glory to Yourself in my body
  and in my spirit.
• Guide me to know the way I am to go.
• Lord, give me a spirit of wisdom, under-
  standing, knowledge, and reverence for You.

Prayers of Intercession

(See week 6.) God is Master, and you are His servant. He is working in the world to reconcile the lost to Himself through Christ. In carrying out Kingdom purposes, God has chosen you to labor with Him. One way to work with God is through prayers of intercession. Intercessory prayers are for God's Kingdom purposes to be completed in the lives of others. Your Master will lead your prayers according to His purposes.

Examples of Intercession

"'LORD, please open his eyes and let him see.' So the LORD opened the servant's eyes. He looked and saw that the mountain was covered with horses and chariots of fire all around Elisha" (2 Kings 6:17).

"LORD God of Abraham, Isaac, and Israel, our ancestors, keep this desire forever in the thoughts of the hearts of Your people, and confirm their hearts toward You" (1 Chronicles 29:18).

Jesus' Intercession

"Holy Father,
protect them by Your name
that You have given Me,
so that they may be one as We are one.
I am not praying
that You take them out of the world
but that You protect them from the evil one.
Sanctify them by the truth;
Your word is truth.
I pray not only for these,
but also for those who believe in Me
through their message.

May they all be one,
as You, Father, are in Me and I am in You.
May they also be one in Us,
so the world may believe You sent Me.
I have given them the glory You have given Me.
May they be one as We are one.
I am in them and You are in Me.
May they be made completely one,
so the world may know You have sent Me
and have loved them as You have loved Me"
(John 17:11,15,17,20-23).

Paul's Intercession

"I pray that He may grant you, according to the riches of His glory, to be strengthened with power through His Spirit in the inner man, and that the Messiah may dwell in your hearts through faith. I pray that you, being rooted and firmly established in love, may be able to comprehend with all the saints what is the breadth and width, height and depth, and to know the Messiah's love that surpasses knowledge, so you may be filled with all the fullness of God" (Ephesians 3:16-19).

"We haven't stopped praying for you. We are asking that you may be filled with the knowledge of His will in all wisdom and spiritual understanding, so that you may walk worthy of the Lord, fully pleasing to Him, bearing fruit in every good work and growing in the knowledge of God. May you be strengthened with all power, according to His glorious might, for all endurance and patience, with joy giving thanks to the Father, who has enabled you to share in the saints' inheritance in the light" (Colossians 1:9-12).

Stephen's Intercession

"He knelt down and cried out with a loud voice, 'Lord, do not charge them with this sin!' And saying this, he fell asleep" (Acts 7:60).

A Church's Example

"Peter was kept in prison, but prayer was being made earnestly to God for him by the church" (Acts 12:5).

Epaphras's Example

"Epaphras … is always contending for you in his prayers, so that you can stand mature and fully assured in everything God wills" (Colossians 4:12).

Possible Requests

- assurance
- Christian fruit
- conviction of sin
- endurance
- faithfulness
- generosity
- hope
- integrity
- judgment
- knowledge
- loyalty
- obedience
- peace
- provision of needs
- right conduct
- spiritual cleansing
- stewardship
- wisdom
- bold witnessing
- Christian unity
- deliverance
- faith
- forgiveness
- holiness
- humility
- joy
- justice
- love
- mercy
- patience
- preservation
- purity
- right motives
- spiritual growth
- understanding

- calling of Christian workers
- filling of the Holy Spirit
- guidance, God's will
- healing—spiritual, emotional, physical
- reconciliation of broken relationships
- repentance and revival among God's people
- spirit of servanthood
- spiritual awakening, conversion of the lost
- surrender and submission to Christ

_____

_____

_____

_____

_____

_____

_____

_____

_____

_____

_____

_____

_____

_____

_____

_____

_____

Daily Requests

Daily	Daily Temporary

Weekly Requests

Sunday

Monday

Weekly Requests

Tuesday

Wednesday

_____   _____
_____   _____
_____   _____
_____   _____
_____   _____
_____   _____
_____   _____
_____   _____
_____   _____
_____   _____
_____   _____
_____   _____
_____   _____
_____   _____
_____   _____
_____   _____
_____   _____
_____   _____
_____   _____
_____   _____

Discipleship Helps • *Pray in Faith*

Weekly Requests

Thursday

Friday/Saturday

_____
_____
_____
_____
_____
_____
_____
_____
_____
_____
_____
_____
_____
_____
_____
_____
_____
_____

1	2	3
7	8	9
13	14	15
19	20	21
25	26	27

4	5	6
10	11	12
16	17	18
22	23	24
28	29	30

Suggestions for Praying Together

1. Acknowledge God's presence and active participation with you in prayer.
2. Use common language rather than church words.
3. Speak for yourself, using *I, me, my,* or *mine* rather than *we, us, our,* or *ours.*
4. Prepare yourselves through prayers of confession, cleansing, and reconciliation.
5. Spend time in prayers of worship, praise, and thanksgiving.
6. Spend the bulk of your time in prayers of petition and intercession. Share requests as you pray rather than spend time at the beginning to list and discuss requests.
7. When time permits, pray until God is finished with you.
8. Pray about one subject at a time.
9. Take turns praying about a subject. Continue on that subject as long as God seems to guide the praying.
10. Be specific in what you ask of God.
11. Ask the Holy Spirit to guide your praying according to God's will. Pay attention to the Holy Spirit's direction for praying.
12. Consider God's viewpoint and give God a reason to answer.
13. Use biblical principles, patterns, and promises to guide your requests.
14. Seek Spirit-guided agreement with others in your prayers.
15. Seek to put yourself in the place of those for whom you are praying so that you can "feel" what they feel.
16. Listen to the prayers of others for direction or answers to your prayers.
17. Respond to the prayers of others.
18. Pray for one another.
19. Consider writing down the subjects for which you have prayed so that you can watch with anticipation for God's answers.
20. When God answers a prayer, remember to thank Him and watch for opportunities to testify to His wonderful work.

Evaluating Group Prayer Sessions

1. At particular times did you sense God's presence in a special way? When and how?
2. Did you spend most of your time in prayer rather than discuss prayer or share prayer requests?
3. Did you take time for confession, praise, worship, and thanksgiving? Was it meaningful or just ritual?
4. Did you pray about one subject at a time, or did individuals tend to pray through a list of several unrelated requests at one time?
5. Were your requests to God specific, or were they general and vague? Will you recognize when God answers your requests?
6. Did you use Bible promises, patterns, examples, or principles in your praying? Were they meaningful or helpful? Have any come to mind after your prayer session that would have been meaningful? If so, share them with the group.
7. Did you give God reasons to answer?
8. Did you come to a sense of Spirit-led agreement about the direction of your requests? Did your faith increase?
9. Did you listen to and respond to others' prayers?
10. Did you pray for one another?

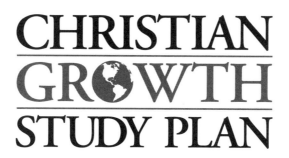

CHRISTIAN GROWTH STUDY PLAN

In the Christian Growth Study Plan *Pray in Faith* is a resource for course credit in the subject area Prayer in the Christian Growth category of diploma plans. To receive credit, read the book; complete the learning activities; attend group sessions; show your work to your pastor, a staff member, or a church leader; then complete the form. This page may be duplicated. Send the completed form to:

Christian Growth Study Plan
One LifeWay Plaza; Nashville, TN 37234-0117
fax (615) 251-5067; e-mail *cgspnet@lifeway.com*
For information about the Christian Growth Study Plan, refer to the current *Christian Growth Study Plan Catalog*, located online at *www.lifeway.com/cgsp*. If you do not have access to the Internet, contact the Christian Growth Study Plan office, (800) 968-5519, for the specific plan you need.

Pray in Faith
COURSE NUMBER: CG–1255

PARTICIPANT INFORMATION

Social Security Number (USA ONLY-optional)

Personal CGSP Number*

Date of Birth (MONTH, DAY, YEAR)

Name (First, Middle, Last)

Home Phone

Address (Street, Route, or P.O. Box)

City, State, or Province

Zip/Postal Code

Email Address for CGSP use

Please check appropriate box: ❑ Resource purchased by church ❑ Resource purchased by self ❑ Other

CHURCH INFORMATION

Church Name

Address (Street, Route, or P.O. Box)

City, State, or Province

Zip/Postal Code

CHANGE REQUEST ONLY

☐ Former Name

☐ Former Address

City, State, or Province

Zip/Postal Code

☐ Former Church

City, State, or Province

Zip/Postal Code

Signature of Pastor, Conference Leader, or Other Church Leader

Date

*New participants are requested but not required to give SS# and date of birth. Existing participants, please give CGSP# when using SS# for the first time. Thereafter, only one ID# is required. **Mail to:** Christian Growth Study Plan, One LifeWay Plaza, Nashville, TN 37234-0117. Fax: (615)251-5067.

Revised 4-05

THE GROWING DISCIPLES SERIES

New and growing believers need a firm foundation on which to build their lives. The Growing Disciples Series provides short-term Bible studies that establish a strong foundation for a life of following Jesus Christ. The series begins with *The Call to Follow Christ*, which introduces six spiritual disciplines. Subsequent studies help believers understand and practice disciplines that strengthen their love relationship with Christ and develop a lifestyle of faithful, fruitful obedience. Watch for the following six-week resources as the series grows:

Growing Disciples: Abide in Christ

Growing Disciples: Live in the Word

Growing Disciples: Pray in Faith

Growing Disciples: Fellowship with Believers

Growing Disciples: Witness to the World

Growing Disciples: Minister to Others

The Call to Follow Christ: Six Disciplines for New and Growing Believers by Claude King is a seven-session, foundational resource that introduces the six disciplines in the series. This unique workbook includes a music CD with seven songs sung by Dámaris Carbaugh that will enrich participants' daily 10- to 15-minute interactive devotion/study time.

Item 001303666

To order these resources and to check availability, fax (615) 251-5933; phone toll free (800) 458-2772; order online at *www.lifeway.com;* e-mail *orderentry@lifeway.com;* visit the LifeWay Christian Store serving you; or write to LifeWay Church Resources Customer Service; One LifeWay Plaza; Nashville, TN 37234-0113.